The Beauty of
Forgiving
and
Forgiveness

Twice Blessed

S. MICHAEL WILCOX

DESERET
BOOK

Salt Lake City, Utah

To Laurie—
For all she forgave

Library of Congress Cataloging-in-Publication Data

Names: Wilcox, S. Michael, author.

Title: Twice blessed : the beauty of forgiving and forgiveness / S. Michael Wilcox.

Description: Salt Lake City, Utah : Deseret Book, [2016] | 2016 | Includes bibliographical references and index.

Identifiers: LCCN 2016012646 | ISBN 9781629721828 (hardbound : alk. paper)

Subjects: LCSH: Forgiveness—Religious aspects—The Church of Jesus Christ of Latter-day Saints. | Forgiveness—Religious aspects—Mormon Church.

Classification: LCC BX8643.F67 W55 2016 | DDC 234/.5—dc23

LC record available at http://lccn.loc.gov/2016012646

Printed in the United States of America
Edwards Brothers Malloy, Ann Arbor, MI

10   9   8   7   6   5   4   3   2   1

Contents

"Be ye therefore merciful, as your Father also is merciful. . . .
Forgive, and ye shall be forgiven:
Give, and it shall be given unto you;
good measure, pressed down, and shaken together, and running over."

LUKE 6:36–38

Fair as the Moon

"And forgive us our debts, as we forgive our debtors."

MATTHEW 6:12

The Most Important Words

I was once very earnestly asked, "What are the three most important phrases a person can say?" The question came with such intensity that I paused before giving my reply. I assumed the phrases would also be the three most important ones to *hear*. Maybe it was a trick question, but it was intriguing enough for me to give some serious thought. I hope I answered correctly. There are certain things we all need to say, to hear, to feel, to know deep down at the soul's center point as critically as we require the Spirit's continuing soft assurances that testify of the gospel, "It's still true." There are certain assurances that are essential to our soul's well-being, perhaps even more crucially so than the calm whisperings of truth that still our hearts and minds of doubts and anxieties. This is a book about one of them.

We never get tired of hearing "the grand three." And we will never reach the point when we need not express them ourselves. We benefit equally in saying and hearing them. We require them daily, both on the receiving and the giving end.

They are part of a healthy soul. I doubt there is much joy in life without them. Their articulation or acknowledgement alone is not enough—they must be felt along the bones and in the veins, wrapped in the warm security of sincerity. They make the mortal journey, with all its uncertainties, dilemmas, disappointments, as well as joy-filled elations, into something understandable—bearable—enjoyable—educative. Each can be stated in three words. They are all so very simple, so plain, that their very obviousness can diminish their necessity, and we may begin to take them for granted. We may say, "Oh, I've heard all that before." Yet, we would do well to pause and consider their importance.

Here are the three phrases with which I answered the question: *I love you. I appreciate you. I forgive you.* To these three ideas we add accompanying words to suit each circumstance in our lives. Love/compassion, appreciation/gratitude, and forgiveness/mercy are all directed toward people, family, humanity, ourselves, and the Divine. They are health and they are healing. They carry with them a natural desire to be expressed. Failure to communicate them usually results in their diminishment. A person with love, gratitude, or forgiveness in his or her heart wants earnestly for the recipient of those feelings to know the sentiments exist. That is one of the ways we know we truly feel them. Over the years I have come to realize that these three sentiments—love, gratitude, and forgiveness—constitute the major themes of scripture and of revealed truth. Almost every story in and out of the scriptures—stories from Genesis to the classics of great literature—center on them. They are life's meaning fulfilled. They are interrelated and somewhat inseparable.

I suppose that in many ways they are overused at the surface level and have somewhat lost their power. The word *love*, for instance, is used to describe our feeling for everything from a slice of pizza to a fashion in clothing to a current TV show. Even our national day of gratitude now seems embarrassingly stuck between Halloween and Christmas.

Gratitude and adoration, love and affection we will leave for another time, but let us move a little deeper into the subject of forgiveness and see what we can discover. Of all the gospel's graces, forgiveness is closest to the Divine heart. There is nothing so fair and beautiful as forgiveness. All the great conflicts of the world have been intensified and passed on to following generations because earlier ones would not forgive. That is a tragic inheritance. Would it not be better to live in the home called "Forgiveness" and never depart?

This is not a book about repentance. That is a topic for its own house, and though forgiveness and repentance are deeply intertwined, we will try to stay focused on the former. There are times when forgiveness is offered or even required *before* repentance, and for our own spiritual health it must exist independent of another's position or actions. One of the most beautiful examples of this is our Savior's plea from the cross, "Father, forgive them; for they know not what they do" (Luke 23:34). This was offered not after the cruelty of crucifixion, but during the very act of the mocking soldiers and gathered crowds. We certainly would not wish to diminish the pillar of repentance in the gospel's temple. I sense in reading Alma's magnificent desire to be an angel and cry repentance to every people that the concept was one of wonder and beauty to him; however, I believe that desire was centered on what would arise out of the change of heart his cry would bring, and that outcome was mercy, healing, and peace—forgiveness.

The Mansion of Forgiving

Upon crossing the threshold of "Mercy's Mansion," almost immediately we see several doors inviting us to ponder what lies behind them, for forgiveness has many rooms within its walls. As I have grown older, some of the rooms have surprised me. Of course they are rooms in the mansion of my own mind and may not have as much relevance to you, but I suspect most are universal. In these quarters I have sat and pondered and reflected. In almost all of these rooms I have experienced failure as well as memorable moments of peace, joy, and wonder.

Let us open some of the doors of these rooms. I have chosen just a few as indicative of the splendor of the whole house. In one we encounter family members, in another our fellow man. In one we sit alone with ourselves. In one the deepest wounds need to be faced. In them all we sense the continual presence of Divinity. We wander down the corridors of the mansion and look at the words above each door. "Clothed in Eden," "This Thy Brother," "Seven Times in a Day," "Bruised Reeds," "Bury Your Weapons," "When the Soul Is Pierced." Within the rooms we learn of such things as "coming near," "releasing the debtor," "seeing the woman," "the winking God," "taking accounts," and "pink people." We sense that sooner or later we will know each room's brightly lit hearths and furnishings. There is also one room we may hesitate to enter because it seems such a contradiction. It is a room we may never personally face but will still enter because so very many do. Here we read the words, "Is There No Pity?" Those who wait in this room struggle to understand or even "forgive" God (if such a thing is not a contradiction) and the world's cruelties. Through all these rooms we learn the lessons first promised in Eden, and our souls expand with the warmth and light of compassion.

Since we all need to be forgiven and all need to bestow forgiveness in kind, at any given time or circumstance in our lives we may enter the rooms either as the receiver or the giver—receiving forgiveness or forgiving another. Mercy faces two ways like the Roman god Janus. What do our minds first think of when the word *forgiveness* is spoken? Does it refer to what I wish to receive from God and others? Does it refer to what I am struggling to accept? Does it refer to what I am laboring to grant? Am I trying to forgive or hoping to be forgiven? Justice can have such a strong hold on our minds that we may be tempted to turn its face outward while wishing for the forgiving, merciful face to turn in our direction. Here the mind may battle the soul, and we will talk of this later. It is good to remember the double perspective of forgiveness or else the topic becomes just another Sunday School discussion. We learn the beauty of pity and pardon—of mercy—because we both sin and are sinned against. William Faulkner wrote in *As I Lay Dying*, "He had a word, too. Love, he called it. But I had been used to words for a long time. . . . People to whom sin is just a matter of words, to them salvation is just words too" (Random House [1985], 164).

That is one of the reasons Jesus "was in all points tempted like as we are." Temptation and the struggles of the human heart were not alien to Him, and He could thus "be touched with the feeling of our infirmities" and "come boldly unto the throne of grace, that we may obtain mercy" (Hebrews 4:15-16). These were not just words to Him. And He certainly had much to forgive within the boundaries of His own life. In our need to receive forgiveness is born the need also to forgive; otherwise it's all just words. For all of us both sin and the need for salvation are realities. Only one man needed no forgiveness, for He never yielded to temptation. This is the wonder of Jesus and His mercy-drawn heart. He was always on the offering end.

As we explore various scriptural accounts, we try to apply the stories to our own lives in the appropriate manner as the Spirit helps us. There are times when we are Joseph who was sold into Egypt and times when we are his brothers. We know what it is to be the Prodigal as well as the older brother, and we pray that we may never lose the heart-vision of the father in that glorious parable, perhaps the most beautiful piece of literature ever written. We usually know what we are seeking when we enter the rooms of forgiveness, and we may ask the Holy Spirit to help us receive the desired or needed encouragement, hope, comfort, assistance, warning, or counsel. Forgiveness is one of the highest mountains we are asked to climb, yet the view is glorious. It can be a hurdle that most stumble over as they run the race of life. But at its core, forgiveness is one of life's most pleasing feelings—that of love, of compassion, of benevolence. It is most sublime in its expression. I believe that love is the nucleus of every soul, and that is why we never really fight the urge that desires to forgive. We want to do it and to do it well. We may not be able to do it because pain can be deep, but we know we must try. It is part of our truest nature, that spiritual being found within. If the desire to forgive fades within us, we are losing part of what it is to be human. Vengeance is the most worthless of causes. Ironically, when forgiveness is most perfect, it is given so freely that one often feels there was never any need for it in the first place. That is part of its spiritually mystic nature.

Most people don't want to talk about forgiveness—they want to feel it, especially if there is an immediate need in their own life. Discussions and diagrams, formulas and formats, lessons and lectures often are of little help. You can't think or will your way into forgiveness. Believe me, I've tried. It seems that the scriptures don't describe forgiveness; they present stories of people who wear one of its faces, and we feel with them. We enter into them and listen to their heartbeats. In the rooms of forgiveness we sit by the fireside, stories are told to us—tales of real people—and the soul is engaged more than the mind. In this way, to borrow the terms used in theatrical tragedy, we experience a catharsis or purging of emotion that helps us with our own situations. Most of us really don't profit much from talking about God or Jesus. We want to experience Their love, think Their thoughts, and see with Their eyes. We want to feel Their involvement in our lives. It is the power of God in operation we seek, not a sermon, whether that power is manifested in prayers answered or in mighty changes of heart. It is the soul we most want touched, not the mind, and this is especially true when considering something so intertwined with the heart as mercy. We want to live in the house, not read descriptions or look at pictures of it. It is the presence of God we so desire, and that can border on the mystical, but it is usually at this level that forgiveness, on both the giving and receiving end, becomes possible and beautiful. Forgiveness is never just indifference, a waiving of penalties or letting someone off the hook and hoping God will do the same for us. Forgiveness is love. It is felt in the soul. It is to replace our way of seeing and feeling with God's way. Being able to forgive others instills within us the assurance that God can and will forgive us. The mercy we feel moving outward carries its own conviction inward. The more we forgive, the more we feel forgiven. We look into the mirror and see our own reflection receiving what we have sent to others. It is that simple.

Moonlight Truths

Forgiveness—along with compassion, mercy, empathy, gratitude—belongs to what I call the "moonlight" truths of the gospel. They are gentle, soft, healing in nature. In the twelfth chapter of the book of Revelation, John saw a beautiful woman who was clothed in three distinct types of light—starlight, sunlight, and moonlight. The woman suggests, through symbolic imagery, God's people, His Church, and His gospel, which shine into the world the Lord's truth, goodness, and beauty. Light and truth are almost always interchangeable in the scriptures. Here is the verse: "And there appeared a great wonder in heaven; a woman clothed with the sun, and the moon under her feet, and upon her head a crown of twelve stars" (Revelation 12:1). As Latter-day Saints we should recognize this order of celestial hierarchy, for it corresponds to the architecture on the outside of many of our temples. I used to think the sun stones, moon stones, and star stones (most prominently seen on the Nauvoo and Salt Lake Temples) represented the three degrees of glory, but I was a bit confused as to their order. Yet when we apply Revelation 12 to the order on the temple, everything fits beautifully. It is true that symbols can represent many things, so it is perfectly fine to think of the three degrees of glory when we look at the stones on the temple, but we don't want to miss the major point. John's focus was on this world, not the next, and the truth that would go forth into it.

In the ancient world people used the stars to navigate, to find their position or set their course. Starlight is guiding, directing light. In Revelation it came from twelve stars. We can interpret these as the apostles and prophets, since this is a New Testament verse. But we could also interpret them as the twelve tribes of Israel, which were chosen or elected to send the Lord's light into the lives of their fellow men. Stars can be used for navigation and for obtaining one's bearings because they are constant. (The planets were called the "wandering" stars since they moved across the night sky's more permanent constellations.) So too are the leaders we follow constant, and they can help us find our way in a world of so very many "wandering" stars—celebrities or personalities whose morals, ethics, and positions shift and change.

We get help in understanding the meaning of the sunlight and moonlight by pondering a verse in the Song of Solomon, which is love poetry between a bridegroom and bride or husband and wife. The man describes the woman he loves with these words: "Who is she that looketh forth as the morning, fair as the moon, clear as the sun" (Song of Solomon 6:10). Part of this verse is quoted three times in the Doctrine and

Covenants as a description of what the Restoration will bring into the world. In two of these modern verses the words are interchanged, allowing the moon to be clear and the sunlight equally fair.

Sunlight is clarifying light, a light that can illuminate every aspect of our lives and our world. We normally do not have to wrestle with many issues, as there is clarification in the gospel to see them with greater understanding and eternal perspectives. We all benefit from light-bearing doctrines, stories, ordinances, and counsel. C. S. Lewis once wrote, "I believe in Christianity as I believe that the sun has risen: not only because I see it, but by it I see everything else" (*The Weight of Glory* [HarperCollins, 2001], 140).

Alma taught the poor of the Zoramites that they would be able to perceive truth through its illuminating quality and they would say: "It beginneth to enlighten my understanding . . . . O then, is not this real? I say unto you, Yea, because it is light; and whatsoever is light, is good, because it is discernible" (Alma 32:28, 35).

This leaves us with the moonlight, which brings us to our topic, that of forgiveness. The word the poet in Song of Solomon used to describe the light of the moon was "fair," and for whatever reason, he mentioned it before the sunlight. We have all watched a full moon and seen the soft shadows it can cast on a cloudless night. There are truths or qualities that are restful, delicate, peace-engendering, subtle, gently beautiful, soothing, and welcoming—to use a word used by Alma the Younger, "delicious" (Alma 32:28). Forgiveness is as fine an example of moonlight reality as I can think of. It flows over the soul. It is the good Samaritan's olive oil, soothing wounds. It is something we all need—both to receive and to give. Yet there is irony in this reality. As wondrous as is moonlight forgiveness, it is sometimes so very hard to give—or receive, for that matter. There is a seeing in forgiveness, however, that like the moon's radiance, is never harsh on the eyes. There is no blinking, no hand-shading view, no turning away when we look directly into the core of its beam. And as they do in the light of the moon, in forgiveness's light, flaws and blemishes of our character are muted and disappear, so gently does it illuminate our souls. Though God sees us in the bright clarifying light of His perfect sun-vision, I sense He loves the moonlight view of His children, for it is so reflective of Him. Let us enter the mansion of forgiveness and explore its rooms—rooms lit by the gentle radiance of God's own love—"fair as the moon."

CHAPTER ONE

Clothed in Eden

Forgiveness from Creation's Dawn

"A tree to be desired to make one wise."

GENESIS 3:6

The Mythopoetic

Genesis was the first revealed scripture God gave to the world. Therein are stories and truths that we might call "first-tier" principles. Given so early in the world's history, they seem to teach those elemental ideals that God would have all His children from the very beginning learn and internalize in their lives. Part of our receiving the healing hope and guidance of these primeval stories, especially that of Adam and Eve, is in our learning how to read them. The earliest chapters of Genesis are not written in the style of writing we may call "historical narrative," but are written in one we can title "mythopoetic." Understanding this is essential. When we read something in the historical-narrative style we anticipate that almost all the elements of the story can be taken at face value and read straightforwardly. The history of David's life and the ministry of Jesus are of this genre. However, when we switch to the mythopoetic, there are other expectations and unique ways of teaching, which are equally valid. It is somewhat counterproductive to read the mythopoetic with the historical-narrative mind. We will miss a great deal and become subject to misunderstanding and sometimes outright foolishness.

We must not be alarmed at the world "myth," which suggests to too many people a story of fiction. In this style, not everything must be read as literally as in historical narrative. The figurative and symbolic come into play. The writing is often driven by imagery and emblematic story. We are aiming at the meaning and truths behind the story—not its details. We are especially invited to deeply relate to the characters in the account, for what happens to them in many cases is archetypal. We must see ourselves in these stories. The personalities and events represent the broad spectrum of humanity. For example, the Creation story is best appreciated when read with the mind-set with which we would read a poem. When read this way, it is more alive, lovelier. The emphasis is on the beauty, variety, and creative genius of God, not a scientific exposition of the grand creative process. "I did it. I did a good job. So love it and take care of it," the Lord tells us in beautiful and repetitive language alive with imagery. This should receive the emphasis, and this accent is what is rightly depicted in the endowment. If we tie the creative process down too sharply, we are going to have difficulties, such as in how the account in Genesis, and even in our modern-day scriptures, differs from that given in the temple. On the poetic level the concern goes away, as the details are secondary to the emotional impact desired.

Naked and Not Ashamed

Such is the story in the Garden of Eden. At first glance this is obvious, as man was not factually made from "the dust of the ground" (Genesis 2:7); woman did not literally arise from the rib or side of a man, and snakes don't talk or walk with legs. We can remember also that we never have to reject or deny the literal when reading this literary style, as both may be in play, but the essential truths are to be found in the figurative. Here is an example in the Adam and Eve story that may serve as a prelude to the one image dealing with forgiveness we want to particularly understand, as it is central to the Lord's purpose in the whole Eden episode. Remember, this is a forgiveness story.

"I, the Lord God, caused a deep sleep to fall upon Adam" (Moses 3:21). *Deep sleep*, when used elsewhere in the Bible, does not mean the person is sleeping as we view sleep. In the case of Abraham (see Genesis 15:12) and Daniel (see Daniel 8:18 or 10:9), for example, the person is in a revelatory state, receiving visions and truths in a celestial environment. Each is fully alert. Of the termination of the First Vision, Joseph Smith wrote, "When I came to myself" (JS—H 1:20), and Paul spoke of a vision he had when he was caught up to the third heaven: "Whether in the body, I cannot tell; or whether out of the body, I cannot tell" (2 Corinthians 12:2). In a manner of speaking, they were both in a state of deep sleep at the time of these revelations. This reading of the description of *deep sleep* highly elevates the moment in the Garden of Eden when Eve, or woman, is introduced onto the stage of creation. I do not wish to make this a treatise on figurative language, but I feel the groundwork needs to be set for the first wonderful teaching given in earth's history of forgiveness, for forgiveness is a dominant theme in this story and it is relevant to us all. We are all Adam. We are all Eve.

We are told both Adam and Eve were "naked . . . and were not ashamed" (Moses 3:25). This could certainly be literal, although we might also say that modesty is an eternal principle. Nonetheless, the beauty and power is in the figurative. In their innocence, Adam and Eve had nothing to hide from each other or God. They had nothing to cover up. They were "not ashamed" because of this, for there was no action that could generate shame. They were innocent and determined to obey all of the Father's commandments. When Lucifer accomplished his aim in getting them both to take of the fruit of the tree of the knowledge of good and evil, we read, "The eyes of them both were opened, and they knew that they had been naked. And they sewed fig leaves together and made themselves aprons" (Moses 4:13). For the fullest insight into this verse we might add as clarification, "They knew that they had been naked—*and had not been ashamed.*" Now they wished to hide, to cover up. Let us not get diverted in the story by doctrinal issues of the necessity of the Fall, or the courage of Eve, or how much they knew or did not know at this moment. We are looking at the story for insight into our own lives and behavior, and that insight comes with the symbolic.

Fruits from the Tree

In a certain sense, the tree of the knowledge of good and evil represents human agency and our mortal state. We exercise agency in response to law and thereby taste the fruits of good and the fruits of evil actions. We learn by our own experience what the consequences of good and evil taste like and can increasingly choose the good. The Lord explained it all to Adam, saying, "They taste the bitter, that they may know to prize the good" (Moses 6:55). That is what the tree is all about. It presents the great opposites—despair and delight, good and evil, virtue and vice, sorrow and joy. These are the fruits our choices produce. The tree stands before each of us, and it stands there all the time. Where can you go to get away from the tree in this life? Though many wish to avoid or deny the consequences of choice, the tree will give its fruits as we pick them—bitter or sweet. What fruits come from good? What fruits come from evil?

Later the Father tells the Son, "The man is *become as one of us* to know good and evil" (Moses 4:28; emphasis added). The core truth of godhood or divinity is the ability to distinguish between all good and all evil choices, with the additional understanding that a god will always choose the good. Godhood is the ultimate and final fruit of the tree, or a perfect knowledge of the fruits of good and evil coupled with perfect choice. This is what we are down here to learn. Once we learn this we can partake of the tree of life and live forever, but in a state of exaltation. Jesus learned it better than any other human being, for His perception was always correct and He consistently chose the fruits of goodness. We, however, are going to make many mistakes as we taste the fruits of this tree that we savor every hour of our lives. Forgiveness will be a constant aspect of life. We will see our nakedness and be ashamed. How we deal with that sense of shame will make all the difference in our mortal progression.

Fig-Leaf Aprons

Adam and Eve, in response to Satan's suggestion, chose to hide—to cover up. "They heard the voice of the Lord God, . . . and Adam and his wife went to hide themselves from the presence of the Lord God" (Moses 4:14). This is a very human response, and we all can relate to it. When you or I exercise our agency and partake of forbidden fruit, or as the Lord taught it, we "taste the bitter, that [we] may know to prize the good," we too feel ashamed and wish to hide or cover up our actions. Examples of this are too numerous to name. We, like Adam and Eve, hear the voice of the Lord God calling to us, and He has many voices to invite us out of our coverts. We perceive our nakedness, sew our fig-leaf aprons, and disappear "amongst the trees of the garden" (Moses 4:14), because often we are not ready for the face-to-face encounter with God and our own actions. There are many types of fig-leaf aprons, and I suppose we are fairly acquainted with them all. We certainly all sew them. Some ways they are most frequently sewn are through telling lies, making excuses, rationalizing, blaming others, hiding in the shadows of self-comforting doubt or intellectual posturing, trying to change the moral landscape to make forbidden things acceptable, etc. There may be as many fig-leaf aprons as there are people to sew them, but God has a better way, as He always does.

Coats of Skins

I assume the Lord's calling to His two beloved children was with a voice of tenderness. He certainly knew where they were hiding and why they had sewn the aprons. In the ensuing conversation they came out of hiding, acknowledged their actions, and waited for the Lord's response. Repentance, in a symbolic, visual sense, is removing the aprons, coming out of hiding, and talking openly, trustingly, and honestly with God—and ourselves, we might add. There are consequences of labor for both the man and the woman, but the main thing to understand is the replacement of the fig-leaf aprons for the coats of skins. "Unto Adam, and also unto his wife, did I, the Lord God, make coats of skins, and clothed them" (Moses 4:27). On the figurative level the coats of skins represent the Lord's way of covering nakedness, His answer to those moments when we are ashamed because we are tasting the bitter and are learning to prize the good fruits of our actions. What is His way? Is it not through sending His Son to the earth to "be filled with mercy, according to the flesh, that he may know according to the flesh how to succor his people according to their infirmities. . . . That he might blot out their transgressions according to the power of his deliverance" (Alma 7:12–13)? If we were to finish the symbolic power and beauty of the coats of skins and what they teach, we might ask, "What animal would be the most appropriate to use to make the coats?" And, "How would one obtain their skins?" We would answer, "A lamb would be most appropriate, for Jesus is the lamb of God." And, "The lamb's sacrifice would enable the covering protection to be obtained."

"You don't need to hide from me," the Father assures us all. "There is no reason to sew aprons. I know your nakedness already and have provided my own covering for you. It is the covering of forgiveness made possible through my love and through the love of my Son's sacrifice." We need never hide from the Lord. We need never justify, blame, rationalize, lie, or pretend that eternal law is not eternal law. God does not wish us to evade Him, fear Him, or fail to trust Him. As did Adam and Eve, we simply respond to our Heavenly Father's voice calling to us, get out of the covering of the trees, remove our aprons, and allow Him to clothe us in His forgiveness—in His Son's atoning sacrifice.

There is also inherent in the two coverings the comparison of the warmth, permanence, and fullness of the skins against the less substantial, perishable nature and thinness of the fig leaves. Every day Adam and Eve put on those coats of skins as a constant reminder that they were covered by the forgiving foresight and eternal design of the Father. They were covered by the Son's life and ever-inviting atoning love and mercy. So it was with our first parents, and so it is with us. From time to time I hear the Lord ask me, "What are you sewing, Mike? Why do you need the fig leaves?" It is always asked with concern, and I hear in His voice the moving toward forgiveness already. I drop my needle, we talk, and I feel again the warmth of that skin covering. We are daily clothed in forgiveness, for we will need it daily, as we are so beautifully shown in the Lord's own house. This we must never forget about ourselves and about all other selves. It was one of the first truths our Father in Heaven wished us to know! Humanity's experience on this planet begins with a choice and the subsequent forgiveness.

CHAPTER TWO

"This Thy Brother"

Forgiveness in the Family

*"His father saw him, and had compassion, and
ran, and fell on his neck, and kissed him."*

LUKE 15:20

Feeling Forgiveness

S ince forgiveness is such an essential obligation of life, we should expect that examples of it would be given in the earliest accounts of scripture. If the Garden of Eden story is at its core a forgiveness-mercy story, others follow suit in the subsequent chapters of scripture. But what kind of forgiveness receives the emphasis of priority? Genesis is a chronicle of family—one family in particular, that of Abraham and his immediate descendants. The writer of their lives was very honest, and we see that even the great patriarchs and matriarchs had a few problems to overcome, both in the challenges of their environment and in their own characters. The initial lessons on forgiveness as found in Genesis could be stated simply: "If others have hurt you, forgive them, especially if they are members of your own family." That is a message everyone can understand. It is a first-tier truth.

I have over the years collected from scripture, history, and great literature stories of forgiveness. They are beautiful and life changing. They range from Tolstoy's *War and Peace* to Greek tragedy; from King Arthur's Round Table to the great epics from India. You will find them in the letters written between Jefferson and Adams and the first performance of Handel's *Messiah*. The concept of forgiveness is particularly dominant in Shakespeare's plays. It is a theme as broad as life and can be discovered everywhere. I have collected these stories because I believe the most effective way to learn how to forgive—or repent, for that matter—is not to listen to explanations of the need to forgive or the steps of repentance. Rather, it is to *feel* forgiveness. (I recognize that in even writing this book I am going against my intuitive instincts somewhat. Please forgive my breach of hypocrisy.) If we find it difficult to feel forgiveness in our own painful situations, we may be able to experience it in the lives and dilemmas of others. There is no more beautiful request in all the prayers of our Savior than, "Father, forgive them; for they know not what they do" (Luke 23:34). He ended His life with forgiveness and forgave even while the act against Him was ongoing. The circumstances of those words make them all the more poignant. I experience forgiveness and mercy deep in my soul every time I read that petition, and with that feeling in my being I can more easily turn His love to my own need to forgive.

In my assemblage of forgiveness stories, I notice that those I love the dearest and that are most effective in stirring my soul in the core of my interior landscape are the accounts involving family. It seems forgiveness is most lovely here. Sadly, for whatever reason, it is sometimes so very hard to forgive those closest to us. But it is also vital, for our well-being and for that of our loved ones, as President Thomas S. Monson teaches: "The spirit must be freed from tethers so strong and feelings never put to rest, so that the lift of life may give buoyancy to the soul. In many families, there are hurt feelings and a reluctance to forgive. It doesn't really matter what the issue was. . . . Only forgiveness heals" ("Hidden Wedges," *Ensign*, May 2002, 19). It seems it is a truism of life that our greatest joys and our greatest hurts come from those we love the most. Hence we perceive the need to learn forgiveness, as we learn almost all our most vital lessons, in the relationships of family—parent-child, brother-sister, husband-wife, and family beyond. So it should not bring any level of amazement that two of the loveliest scenes of forgiveness are given early to us and that they are found in the most family-oriented book of scripture—Genesis.

"And Esau Ran to Meet Him"

I don't think we need to rehearse all the details of the relationship of Jacob and Esau. In our studies and discussions we spend a great deal of time either condemning or justifying Jacob and Esau, either for selling a sacred birthright for a mess of pottage or for deceptively fooling a blind Isaac in order to receive a father's blessing. It is difficult not to feel empathy for Esau as he pleads with his father for a blessing upon his own head. "He cried with a great and exceeding bitter cry, and said unto his father, Bless me, even me also, O my father. . . . Hast thou not reserved a blessing for me? . . . Hast thou but one blessing, my father? bless me, even me also, O my father. And Esau lifted up his voice, and wept" (Genesis 27:34, 36, 38).

Esau goes right into the empathy of my heart every time I read those words.

However, his method of dealing with his brother turns harsh when he plots to kill Jacob as soon as Isaac is dead, an event that he thinks is soon approaching. So Rebekah sends her favored son to her brother Laban to find a wife among his daughters, anticipating that Esau's anger will cool given time and the opportunity to see how his own behavior has caused the loss of his blessing at least as much as, if not more than, his brother's and mother's subterfuge. This realization is an essential part of his ability to forgive, and it is equally true of our own. When we continually focus on the wrongs other members of the family or broader society have inflicted on us, the unfairness, the pain, the humiliation of it all can make it so difficult to move forward into compassion. Forgiveness is rarely about others. We forgive for our own spiritual welfare. Self-reflection is always an early step to healing, and forgiveness is the soul's sweetest healing. Notice the inward turning manifested in Esau's thoughts as he watches his brother Jacob leaving for Laban's country to find a covenant wife, something Esau has failed to do in his own marriage: "When Esau saw that Isaac had blessed Jacob, and sent him away to Padanaram, to take him a wife from thence; and that as he blessed him he gave him a charge, saying, Thou shalt not take a wife of the daughters of Canaan; and that Jacob obeyed his father and his mother, and was gone to Padan-aram; and Esau seeing that the daughters of Canaan pleased not Isaac his father; then went Esau unto Ishmael, and took unto the wives which he had Mahalath the daughter of Ishmael Abraham's son"

(Genesis 28:6-9). He is trying to make amends to his parents for earlier choices he knows displeased them.

There is a second truth I love in this story, which contributes to the beautiful scene we will soon witness between these two brothers. I know not what to call this principle other than "Time's Pushing Back." There are times in our lives when we want to forgive. God asks us to, and we wish to honor Him and let go of the pain, but the ability to do so at the moment is lacking. Time helps because it pushes back the memory and replaces it with other things to fill the vision so that the hurt is not so dominant in our view. We push the pain back with good memories. It may not look so daunting from a distance. If those positive memories involve the person in question, all the better—but many times that cannot be. Nevertheless, "Time's Pushing Back" is a forceful healer even though it is often so clichéd. This force, however, will not work if we continually dwell on the injury instead of the positive things that separate where we are now and what happened in the past. We can make the past a perpetual present if we are not careful. How many years transpire before the brothers in our story meet again in an embrace trumped only by the Savior's own tale of the Prodigal Son? Jacob labored seven years for Rachel. He is then deceived himself, marrying Leah instead as one sibling again replaces another. There is a little poetic irony in this. One week later his beloved Rachel is his, but he must toil for another seven years. When those years are over he then works six more years to obtain his flocks and herds before sensing by Laban's attitude toward him and the inner stirrings of the Spirit that it is time to go home. That's twenty years in total. What has happened to Esau's anger and plotting in the meanwhile?

On the return, Jacob sends messengers to Esau, telling him, "Thy servant Jacob saith thus . . . I have sent to tell my lord, that I may find grace in thy sight" (Genesis 32:4-5). When the messengers return, they inform Jacob that his brother is coming with four hundred men. Jacob is convinced they are coming to destroy him. His assumption about his brother is severe—thinking Esau will kill his wives and children also. How often we make similar suppositions about the reactions of those whose forgiveness or reconciliation we seek, and this may hold us back. Jacob's fears (we may add that they are false fears) cause him to plead fervently with the Lord and "wrestle" all night long seeking God's blessing. The wrestling is certainly good in and of itself, as it is always beneficial to pray soul-deep, but it is not needed in this instance because Esau is not coming to destroy. He is approaching to greet in love and affection. He is coming to forgive and seek forgiveness. This is his twin brother, after all.

As the brothers approach each other, Jacob bows seven times, and then we read, "And Esau ran to meet him, and embraced him, and fell on his neck, and kissed him: and they wept" (Genesis 33:4). Please visualize this scene. It rarely fails to move me to tears, and I feel forgiveness in the marrow of my bones. This is surely the one critically vital moment we are to remember in the lives of these two brothers. Forget the mess of pottage, forget the goats' skins on Jacob's arms kneeling before his blind father, Isaac, forget every other detail in the story of Genesis as it regards this family, but never forget this scene. It is one of the climactic moments of Genesis, and all the other events and details of the story are but preludes to this wondrous sight. I would point out that Jesus Himself used the same description in that Everest-high parable, the Prodigal Son, when the father greets his returning son (see Luke 15:20).

When Jacob attempts to give a generous gift to his brother, Esau simply replies, "I have enough, *my brother*; keep that thou hast unto thyself" (Genesis 33:9; emphasis added). Once again, the words *my brother* fill us with the emotions of forgiveness and have the powerful effect of softening the heart as it is directed to the objects of our own difficulties. I repeat, one of the ways we learn to forgive is by feeling forgiveness, by seeing it operate in others' lives, by sensing the poignancy and beauty of it in the embrace, the tears, and the "my brother" of this magnificent reconciliation. There follows a gracious conversation of concern, each brother for the other, and then they part. But the story has one final vista. When Isaac dies and the time comes for the consequences of birthright to be fully in operation, it is Esau who takes "his wives, and his sons, and his daughters, and all the persons of his house, and his cattle, and all his beasts, and all his substance, which he had got in the land of Canaan; and went into the country from the face of his brother Jacob. For their riches were more than that they might dwell together" (Genesis 36:6–7). How easily the major cause of conflict was finally settled. If any-one ever wondered what Esau's state is before his Father in Heaven, this moment should silence all questions. He could certainly, for the rest of his life, pray: "Forgive me my debts, *as I forgave my brother*" (see Matthew 6:12), and his prayer would have been honored. We will return to this story presently, but let us first explore Jacob's sons.

"All His Brethren Hated Him"

We are not even one single chapter past the story of Jacob and Esau before the next episode of family forgiveness is presented. In chapter 37 of Genesis, the story of Joseph and his brothers is introduced. It is as if the Lord is saying to us, "I know how hard forgiveness can be, but it is essential my children learn the release of forgiveness, especially as it comes within families. It is one of the sweet fruits on the tree of the knowledge of good and evil. I am going to give you another story with another scene of reconciliation as a second witness. You will see forgiveness again and feel its joy and beauty; thereby your own ability to forgive will be increased."

The animosity and jealousy between Joseph and his brothers begins before any of them are born. Therein is a principle of life that plays such an important role in this great scriptural theme. In so very many instances in life, from the individual to the national and international levels, one generation creates and passes on the divisions and animosities of their own lives. There are injuries instigated by earlier generations that we must try to forgive and end in our own. The night Laban replaces Rachel with Leah begins the process that leads to one of the saddest moments in Genesis—the sale of Joseph into slavery by his brothers. That is a sin large enough to hang mercy on. I suppose that even in this story Joseph can bear some of the blame for his brothers' dislike. Sharing his

God-given dreams, despite whatever he hoped to accomplish, is somewhat counterproductive.

Let us try to imagine, however, what it was like to live in this family. In a legal, cultural, letter-of-the-law sense, Leah's oldest son would be the destined leader of the family and hold the birthright position because Leah married Jacob first. But in Jacob's mind, it was Rachel he labored for and loved. *Her* son should occupy this position, and Jacob is not going to allow Laban's and Leah's (for she was in agreement) deception to deny Rachel the place he believes she and her sons should hold. Rachel, not Leah, in Jacob's sense of justice, was the first wife. Though the account tells us Jacob loved Joseph more than the other boys, the giving of the coat of many colors was not just an act of favoritism, but a statement that Joseph, as the firstborn son of Rachel, the first wife in Jacob's mind, was to inherit the birthright promises of responsibility and leadership. As the boys are born and grow, their very names hold the hostility beginning to form and grow within the family. Leah's sons were named to show her state of mind and the struggle between the three adults. *Reuben* means, "Look, a son!" causing Leah to remark, "Now therefore my husband will love me." At Simeon's birth she states, "Because the Lord hath heard that I was hated, he hath therefore given me this son also." Levi is next, eliciting from Leah the hope, "Now this time will my husband be joined unto me." Judah, her fourth son, brings the simple statement, "Now will I praise the Lord" (Genesis 29:32–35). Leah is in a difficult position, and we feel her pain and rejection. What impact will this have on her sons? Their very names reflect the tensions within the family.

Rachel, seeing her own barrenness, gives Bilhah to Jacob. Bilhah bears Dan and Naphtali, and Rachel proclaims, "God hath judged me, and hath also heard my voice. . . . With great wrestlings have I wrestled with my sister, and I have prevailed" (Genesis 30:6, 8). Leah counters by giving Zilpah to Jacob, and two more sons are born, Gad and Asher. "A troop cometh," Leah triumphantly points out to her sister, and, "Happy am I, for the daughters will call me blessed" (Genesis 30:11, 13). We read of a confrontation between the two sisters over some mandrakes, which were believed to help infertile women. Here Leah accuses Rachel, "Is it a small matter that thou hast taken my husband?" (Genesis 30:15). You can feel the tensions in the family—tensions, I repeat, that are inherent in the very names of each son. Leah has two more sons, Issachar and Zebulun, certain at last that "now will my husband dwell with me" (Genesis 30:20). Rachel's anguished cry to Jacob, "Give me children, or else I die" (Genesis 30:1), opens her heart to us with the final irony that it will be childbirth that takes her young life. Finally, a somewhat subdued Rachel bears Joseph, saying, "God hath taken away my reproach," and including her hope, "The Lord shall add to me another son" (Genesis 30:23-24).

By that time a great deal of water has passed under the bridge. The long looked-for son is born with the weight of Laban's decision and the two sisters' divisions upon him. The death of his mother in giving birth to Benjamin isolates him even further, and he grows up in an environment where "all his brethren . . . hated him, and could not speak peaceably unto him" (Genesis 37:4). One definition of *wisdom* is the ability to see into the future how our decisions will impact ourselves and others—certainly our family—many generations beyond our own more present-oriented perspective. It is a vision that would prevent much misery and the need for increasingly difficult forgiveness to be given. Unfortunately, Laban did not so perceive.

In our modern language, we might say this is somewhat of a dysfunctional family, and perhaps only Leah could look at herself and say, "I bear some responsibility for initiating the problems." All the rest—including Jacob, we might add—inherit their portion. They might not have dealt with it as graciously as they could have, but they were not the authors of the tension. Life can be unfair, as we all know, and simply acknowledging its inequities helps very little. So Joseph is sold and enters long years of bondage, false accusations, and unfulfilled hopes and dreams. Only Reuben is not complicit in the plot, but undoubtedly spends long years in self-accusation that he had not been more bold in his confrontation with his brothers that they "lay no hand upon him" (Genesis 37:22).

Coming Near

We now move the action of this family tragedy forward two decades. Joseph was seventeen when he was sold and thirty when he interpreted Pharaoh's dream. Thirteen lost years. If we add the seven years of plenty and the one year of famine, Joseph has not seen his family for twenty-one years. What must have been his thoughts as the ten brothers came before him and knew him not? Yet the past action of betrayal has been weighing on them. They have lived twenty-one years with their father's grief, knowing they are its cause, and we must give them the benefit of the doubt that there is great regret over the action of one afternoon. This, however, Joseph does not know yet. When accused by Joseph of being spies, the brothers' first thought links their present danger to that act twenty-one years ago: "We are verily guilty concerning our brother, in that we saw the anguish of his soul, when he besought us, and we would not hear; therefore is this distress come upon us" (Genesis 42:21).

And now the beauty begins to surface—the beauty of growing forgiveness as Joseph "turned himself about from them, and wept" (Genesis 42:24). No wonder the Lord wished this story to be preserved down the ages. There is no desire for revenge, no gloating at his brothers' obvious guilt, no joy in their fears or distress. He responds with tears and then, turning back to his brothers, gives them the chance to redeem themselves in a unique manner. He keeps Simeon and demands they return with their youngest brother, Benjamin, Rachel's last child, who is the son now central in Jacob's affections. The narrative continues to the placing of Joseph's cup in Benjamin's sack of grain. What will the brothers do? They now have a perfect opportunity to abandon Rachel's final son, but Judah movingly pleads for his youngest brother, offering himself as the ransom, painfully aware that his own failure to return will not be as cataclysmic on his father as that of Benjamin. "For how shall I go up to my father, and the lad be not with me? lest peradventure I see the evil that shall come on my father" (Genesis 44:34). Judah has already seen the effect the loss of a son has had on his father by being complicit in Joseph's sale into Egypt. Joseph has given his brothers a wonderful gift—the chance to know that they have truly turned from their former actions. This is part of his for-giveness, part of "loosing" the debt, as we will discuss in the next chapter. The brothers yielded once to the family's major difficulty. They will not do so again!

"Then Joseph could not refrain himself . . . and he cried, Cause every man to go out from me. And there stood no man with him, while Joseph made himself known unto his brethren. And he wept aloud. . . . and Joseph said unto his brethren, I am Joseph; doth my father yet live?" Put yourself in the position of his brothers. How would you respond? What emotions would run through you at such a time? Yet the feel-ing the Lord would have us receive here is the joy of forgive-ness—its sheer loveliness, radiating with divine holiness. "His brethren could not answer him; for they were troubled at his presence. And Joseph said unto his brethren, *Come near to me,* I pray you. *And they came near.* And he said, I am Joseph your brother, whom ye sold into Egypt. Now therefore be not grieved, nor angry with yourselves, that ye sold me hither: for God did send me before you to preserve life. . . . So now it was not you that sent me hither, but God" (Genesis 45:1–5, 8; emphasis added). I know of no more gracious reply in scrip-ture to match this moment. All those years! All that pain! Joseph knows only Judah's pleading. His brothers have yet to say a word of apology. But none is expected or required. It is the "remember them no more" (D&C 58:42) and the "not be mentioned" (Ezekiel 18:22) moment. "Come near to me." Such a magnificent, gentle invitation! Joseph allows us to feel what deep forgiveness is like. How could the brothers not ap-proach? There is such sweetness in those four words, and in these: "And they came near." That is what family forgiveness is all about—*coming near*. How did Joseph do it? If there is forgiveness without the "coming near," is there truly forgiveness or just a waiving of past offenses? I believe forgiveness almost always brings with it the "coming near." It is that extra step that acquaints us with the soul of God.

I assume Joseph had a loving soul, but other factors helped him. God had compensated for the troubled years. We see that in his words to his brothers but also in the names he gives his two sons, Manasseh and Ephraim—one meaning "to forget" and the other "to be fruitful." On the day of their birth Joseph said, "God . . . hath made me forget all my toil, and all my father's house. . . . God hath caused me to be fruitful in the land of my affliction" (Genesis 41:51–52).

"In thy childhood," Lehi told his son Jacob before he died, "thou hast suffered afflictions and much sorrow, because of the rudeness of thy brethren. Nevertheless . . . thou knowest the greatness of God; and he shall consecrate thine afflictions for thy gain" (2 Nephi 2:1–2). In the case of Joseph and in the case of the Book of Mormon's Jacob, affliction was for the family's gain and ultimate survival. That is God's way.

The principle of "coming near" is also seen in Jacob and Esau's embrace. Notice the repetition as Jacob's family approaches the long-feared Esau. "And [Jacob] passed over before them, and bowed himself to the ground seven times, until he *came near* to his brother. . . . Then the handmaidens *came near*, they and their children. . . . And Leah also with her children *came near* . . . and after *came Joseph near* and Rachel" (Genesis 33:3, 6–7; emphasis added). Four times we read the words "came near." I am aware that in both

Joseph's and Jacob's stories the words mean simply that they approached, but let us give them the deeper meaning of spiritual and emotional retying of family relationships. In families, forgiveness—especially the "coming near"—may be the fulfillment of mercy. Our invitation to family members to come near, inasmuch as that nearness does not continue to create harm, becomes the completing action to full forgiveness. We can say, "I forgive you." Can we also say, "Come near to me"? Is not the ultimate "coming near" the essence of the Atonement?—Jesus initiating, facilitating, inviting all of us to come near the Father into eternal felicity?

Friends Again at Last

The Prophet Joseph Smith gives us a lovely example of "coming near" during the Missouri persecutions. This story has become a classic in LDS Church history. William W. Phelps had turned against Joseph, contributing to his incarceration in Liberty Jail. This betrayal was particularly painful. As Joseph would later say of Brother Phelps's defection, "The cup of gall, already full enough for mortals to drink, was indeed filled to overflowing when you turned against us" (*History of the Church of Jesus Christ of Latter-day Saints*, 7 vols. [1932–51], 4:163).

Later William W. Phelps had second thoughts and sought unity once again with his old friend. In a poignant letter to Joseph he asked for forgiveness and more—the opportunity to "come near" in fellowship. "I know my situation, you know it, and God knows it, and I want to be saved if my friends will help me. . . . I ask forgiveness in the name of Jesus Christ of all the Saints. . . . *I want your fellowship; if you cannot grant that,* grant me your peace and friendship, for we are brethren, and our communion used to be sweet" (*History of the Church*, 4:142; emphasis added). In Phelps's mind there was a difference between friendship and fellowship. I believe he is right. Forgiveness alone would bring peace, but it was the "coming near" of fellowship and its sweetness that he so much desired.

The Prophet quickly replied in his own letter. "Believing your confession to be real, and your repentance genuine, I shall be happy once again to give you the right hand of fellowship, and rejoice over the returning prodigal." Joseph then attached a closing two-line poem since William W. Phelps had a poet's heart and they sometimes communicated in verse. It was his way of assuring Phelps that the "coming near" was desired by Joseph as well. He would give both the friendship and the fellowship.

> Come on, dear brother, since the war is past,
> For friends at first, are friends again at last.
> Yours as ever,
> Joseph Smith Jun.
> (*History of the Church*, 4:164)

"Coming near" can be so very, very beautiful. I grew up in a divorced family. In past years we had what was called, somewhat unfeelingly, a "broken home." In my personal life God healed the pain of being left by my own father when I was one year old and the many years when he had virtually nothing to do with his children. Heavenly Father did this by asking me a single question. It came years later, when I was myself a father of sons and knew a father's joys. I could not have understood it earlier. "Would you be the son who lost his father? Or the father who lost his son?" He asked me. It was an invitation to "come near," and I could not refuse it. I too wept long when that question was offered. I wept because I knew, better than my own father had known, all he had missed in life, all the sharing and love. I knew the tragedy of his life. What a release was given me that day.

We are told Joseph wept when he was sold by his siblings, had anguish of soul, and begged for release of his unhearing brothers, but *their* future tears and anguish and pleading were the more painful. Joseph understood this and wept for their pain just as God the Father wept at the suffering of His children in the great vision of Enoch recorded in Moses 7, when He invited Enoch to weep with Him. If we can be the other person, feel that person's pain, stand outside ourselves and next to the offender, forgiveness flows so very naturally in most cases. And with it, we "come near."

With the release of God's question came an urging to invite my father into my life. This invitation was key to his moving through the various processes of repentance in his own life to help him remove years of guilt and self-condemnation. It was a catalyst for changes, which brought release, and a wonderful bishop facilitated those changes. In the following years Laurie and I included him in all the family gatherings, and he knew the simple joys of grandchildren. There were Sunday dinners and birthday candles and Halloween costumes, Christmas mornings and vacations with the family in the tent trailer. In time my father returned to activity in the Church and served a mission on Temple Square and weekly in the temple. None of these things would have happened had the forgiveness been solely the removal of negative or painful feelings in the heart, and, of course, they may not have been possible if I had believed my father's nearness to my family would have caused continuing pain, but in this case all was healing and increased love. The invitation to "come near" and form a relationship was the critical aspect of forgiveness for my father and me. The Lord knew this and taught us all—father, son, and grandchildren—the deepest meaning of His so very powerful stories of forgiveness in Genesis.

Seeing Far

If we look more closely at the Father's weeping in Enoch's vision, a key to forgiveness is given. It is found in the tense the Father uses when describing the people of Noah's generation who would be destroyed in the floods. It teaches us that *part of coming near is the ability to see far.* There was much to forgive in this generation, for the Lord described them with these words: "Among all the workmanship of mine hands there has not been so great wickedness as among thy brethren" (Moses 7:36). Then He adds the bitterness that will come to them because they chose the wrong fruits on the tree of knowledge. It is all in the future tense: "Satan *shall* be their father, and misery *shall* be their doom; and the whole heavens *shall* weep over them . . . wherefore should not the heavens weep, seeing these *shall* suffer?" That suffering would continue until "my Chosen *shall* return unto me, and until that day they *shall* be in torment; wherefore, for this *shall* the heavens weep" (Moses 7:37, 39-40; emphasis added). The understanding of future pain that would ultimately come to his brethren when they re- alized, as everyone will, the cost of their actions, brought tears to Enoch's eyes as he "wept and stretched forth his arms, and his heart swelled wide as eternity" (Moses 7:41).

I suppose we can let the thought of future pain on an offender bring a type of comfort of justice finally being satisfied, but that does not seem to be the Lord's emphasis, and it should not be ours. It was compassion for that suffering that caused both the Father and Enoch to weep. Jacob told the Nephites of his generation that one day "we shall have a perfect knowledge of all our guilt, . . . and our nakedness." All the fig-leaf aprons are gone. There is now nowhere to hide. We shall also have a "perfect knowledge of [our] enjoyment, and . . . righteousness" (2 Nephi 9:14). I assume what Jacob meant by a "perfect knowledge" is that people will know how their actions for good or evil impacted the lives of others on a much more comprehensive level. They will walk in our shoes and know our wounds, wounds they caused, as if they were their own. We will also understand that in regard to our own actions. I believe the Savior covers that knowledge if we allow Him to. That was part of the anguish of His "hour." If we can look into the future, into the *"shall* suffer" and the *"shall* be in torment" days, and let compassion and sorrow arise, we will have come a long way into acquiring the heart and mind of our Father in Heaven. We will be able to forgive. Our *seeing far* will help us *come near.*

I enjoyed a very sweet "come near" moment one afternoon while participating in sealings in the Jordan River Utah Temple. We were sealing members of families from our ancestry. My daughter and I had found their names while searching old wills and censuses. Some questions arose in my mind as I sat there watching the uniting of husband to wife and parent to child. It was not the first time I had pondered these particular questions. Only this time I received an answer. What were their relationships like in life? Did they carry pains inflicted upon one another or loving trust? Was there joy or resentment, peace or hostility? Had there been divorces, rebellious children, neglectful parents, cessation of contact and conversation, financial traumas, or was all in harmony, all full of gratitude for loving, supportive, relationships? I think there are no more beautiful words in all the ordinances of the restored gospel that can match those said in the sealing rooms of the temples when at the altars families are eternally formed—husband and wife, parents and children. I love these words so deeply. When I knelt there for myself with my own wife, Laurie, they represented the summit of this life's happiness, the greatest moment of my life, the best blessing in a life of God-given bests. What had mortality been like for my ancestors, who were now more to me than a name on a census? The answer from the Spirit came so quietly and with a few very simple words. *There is much forgiveness here.* I believe they were the words of my own ancestors, for I have learned that I receive greater insights in the temple when doing work for my own family. That was a comforting thought. Perhaps in the relationships of mortal life there was alienation, but eternity offers the highest "coming near." Perhaps, in some circumstances, it offers the only possibility of final reconciliation and peace.

Laurie and I had few disagreements in our relationship largely because she was so easy to live with, but we both remember what we came to call "the bedspread argument." It was nearing Laurie's birthday, and she wanted a new bedspread for the master bedroom. We went to the mall a few days before her birthday, picked out one she liked, and I bought it. Now in my male mind my birthday duty to my wife was over, but in her female mind I needed to take her out to dinner on the actual day. She dropped enough hints, which I caught but did not wish to acknowledge. We all know how these things start. I was insensitive and she overreacted, as we used to say. Things were said beyond the immediate dispute and we were both hurt, expecting the other person to apologize. We were both in the right in our minds. In the intensity of our discussion, I said, "Well, I will never make that mistake again!" I do not remember what comment she made immediately prior to this, but she interpreted my words to mean I would never buy her another present. The very memory of her confusion fills my soul to this day with empathy and a miniature grieving and agony.

She grew very quiet and I thought the event was over, but I found her later crying. I was still a bit animated from the argument and somewhat annoyed, but it all melted into nothingness when she said poignantly, "You said you'd never give me another present." In that moment, I was not Michael Wilcox, but Laurie Wilcox. I felt her pain. Though it was a misunderstanding, I knew how much it hurt her. It was my hurt now. My seeing far was into the depths of her soul. It brought a "come near" moment.

Family forgiveness becomes so simple if we can just sit in the other chair and feel the soul of the person we love and have hurt or who has hurt us, or turn our vision to a future day. It no longer mattered who was right or wrong, and there was nothing to forgive on either side. That was understood. I said, "I will always buy you a birthday present, Laurie, always!" That was the end. It reached its conclusion in tears, both of ours, and we came near.

"Rejoice with Me"

But there is more to forgiveness than tears. Forgiveness always brings joy; that joy is best felt in reading Jesus' own most beloved parable, that of the Prodigal Son. This also is a family affair. It was directed primarily to those who needed most to hear its soothing message—"all the publicans and sinners" who, we read, "*drew near* unto him . . . to hear him" (Luke 15:1; emphasis added). Notice we are still in the realms of drawing people near with the spirit of forgiveness. Jesus was forgiveness itself—a living personification of all God means for us to attain. The answer to sin is not solely about repentance but also about forgiveness and mercy. Jesus came with that answer just as the Buddha came to teach that the answer to suffering is compassion. When the Pharisees and scribes complained that Jesus was eating with sinners, the sensitivity of Jesus for others' feelings was touched. He was so often troubled in spirit when unkind, hurtful, or judgmental statements were made. That was part of His character. He would tell the parable and its two prelude parables for the complainers also, but I sense His concern was centered on the souls struggling to come back because they discerned in the Master no condemnation. He needed to reassure them of the power of forgiveness lest the murmuring criticism of the Pharisees turn them away again. He would tell the stories for those who needed the healing peace of assured mercy.

Joy is the commanding emotion detailed in Luke chapter 15. It is the emotion Jesus wishes both the sinners and listening Pharisees to feel. I sense no condemnation in Luke 15 even for the judgers. It is a chapter devoted to forgiving joy and compassion, and forgiving joy and compassion alone. It is the emotion we will feel as we read it in the spirit in which it was presented. Jesus introduced the Prodigal Son with the Lost Sheep and Lost Coin parables—one centered in a man's world and one in a woman's. When the lost sheep is found, "He layeth it on his shoulders, *rejoicing.* And when he cometh home, he calleth together his friends and neighbours, saying unto them, *Rejoice with me*; for I have found my sheep which was lost." Jesus then compares this earthly joy to the "*joy . . . in heaven* over one sinner that repenteth." He speaks of "*more*" joy in the lost soul than the "ninety and nine just persons" (Luke 15:5–7; emphasis added). I sense no need to enter discussions of comparable rejoicing. No one need feel threatened. With the "one" there is an *intensity of joy*—with the "ninety and nine" there is a *constancy of joy.* The first joy is celebratory in nature; the second calm and comforting. This we learn when the father in the coming parable tells his oldest son, his "ninety-and-nine" child, "Son, thou art ever with me" (Luke 15:31). The joys are equal in a sense, though of differing qualities. Likewise, *joy* is the key word in the Lost Coin. The woman sweeps her house diligently until she finds the precious coin and then "calleth her friends and her neighbours together, saying, *Rejoice with me.*" Changing the wording as He shifts the scene to heaven, Jesus applies the story to the inhabitants of heaven, not the location of heaven: "Likewise . . . there *is joy in the presence of the angels of God* over one sinner who repenteth" (Luke 15:9–10;

emphasis added). Both God and those with Him rejoice. We would be part of that company in that place, and the spirit of forgiveness puts us there—as I so wonderfully learned in the temple when the Spirit said, "There is much forgiveness here." The invitation to be part of the celebratory joy now comes.

From Husks to the Fatted Calf

This brings us to the Prodigal Son. In this parable, which role do we play? Are we the guilt-dominated, wasting prodigal, who is realizing that the "far country," the world, Babylon, takes everything from you and gives nothing in return, leaving you "in want," feeding the swine? "And no man gave unto him," so he sits among the "husks" with the pigs and thinks of home (Luke 15:13–16). I think we have all eaten a few "husks" in our lifetimes. I certainly have. I believe one of the most powerful lessons of the parable is the son's belief that he could at least go home. Before the need arises, the foundation of family forgiveness is laid in a multiplicity of loving memories that draw the family back into oneness. The groundwork of a loving father was paying off. I know a family who lost a son to the wasted living of the far country. They did not know where he was for months on end. But one Sunday afternoon while he was heating a can of beans over an open fire in the canyons—his meal of husks—the memory of all the family dinners he had shared during his youth on Sunday afternoons touched him. He knew that at that very moment the family would be gathered around the table with an empty chair for him. That was enough. He doused the fire and walked home, took his seat, and was served by his mother. No one said anything. He was home. Something as simple as a Sunday meal was the key. In a mature family, a mature marriage, the memories of the happy loving times give us the ability to go on loving each other when we may not like each other—to hold on until we fall in love again, until trust and respect are reestablished. We stay committed to each other through the hard times with full faith that they do end and that the affection and unity we once felt will be renewed.

In the Savior's parable, the straying son's own sense of self would not allow him to return as a son, but he just wanted to be home. Being a servant would be sufficient. And so "he arose, and came to his father. But when he was yet a great way off, his father saw him, and had compassion, and ran, and fell on his neck, and kissed him" (Luke 15:20). I believe that is the most beautiful verse in the New Testament. The father does not know why the son is returning but runs in welcome nonetheless, just as Joseph wept at the early sight of his brothers' distress and Esau embraced his brother before any words of regret or sorrow for the past escaped Jacob's lips. There is only love and joy. This is no grudging allowance, but not-to-be-mentioned, remembered-no-more forgiveness. "But the father said to his servants, Bring forth the best robe, and put it on him; and put a ring on his hand, and shoes on his feet: and bring hither the fatted calf, and kill it; and let us eat, and be merry: For this my son was dead, and is alive again; he was lost, and is found" (Luke 15:22–24). The son has moved from the husks to the fatted calf. Part of forgiveness is to help returning prodigals realize they are still wanted at the feast. The parable is designed to answer the question, "When you return, do you 'come near' as a servant or a son?" There are no servants in the kingdom, only sons, the Savior answers. And it is the father whose coming near is preceded by running "when he was yet a great way off." That was a beautiful invitation that needed no words.

I have seen, and I am sure you have also, how sad family conflicts can be. Sometimes they arise out of financial concerns—inheritances or business deals gone wrong. They come from differing lifestyles and choices. They develop due to our personalities; parents can be too harsh or children can break mothers' and fathers' hearts in rebellion. Family members cease talking to each other, harmony breaks down, sides are chosen, pride sets in, and years can come and go. We want to hold other family members responsible for the breakdown in relationships. We feel a need to be "right." Our anger or resentment or self-pity must be maintained because that proves we are right. There is a type of revenge in this, the only satisfaction we may get—so we hold on. Maybe we are right, but that only maintains the hostility forever circling the racetrack of the mind. There is a natural gravitational pull in the heart that wants justice—by that I mean, we want it for the other person. For ourselves, we prefer mercy. God is surely on our side, but sometimes I think the Lord may say in loving tenderness, "I can't help you until you realize that in some ways you deserve each other." I'm sure He says it of nations. Forget the need to be right. Forgiveness rises above such thinking. Forgiveness really has very little to do with the other person; it is the invitation to change ourselves in a profound way and become more like the God we worship. Foster the need to be loving. Mortality is not fair. It never will be—that is part of the learning that schools the soul into patterns where we see the

Savior in our own countenances. Perhaps it was these reasons and others even more difficult to forgive, such as abuse, infidelity, cruelty, and neglect, that caused the Savior to choose the family as the setting for His supreme parable. We will enter the room of deep pain and abusive injury in a latter chapter, for these wounds can drain the heart. For now, if we can run toward the "coming near," we are likely to experience the grand joy of the father of the prodigal.

George MacDonald, that loving Scottish minister, once said of parables that they were not told by the Savior for doctrinal reasons. In truth, one of the greatest ways to cloud their meaning is "to interpret rather than do them." They were shared to help create the state of soul whereby the desired emotion is sparked and the necessary action, thought, or attitude is created or renewed. "There is a thing wonderful and admirable in the parables. . . . They are addressed to the conscience and not to the intellect, to the will and not to the imagination. They are not meant to explain anything, but to rouse a man to the feeling, 'I am not what I ought to be, I do not the thing I ought to do'" (*Unspoken Sermons* [Bibliobazaar, 2006], 181). We must not be sidetracked from the power of the story by mingling it with questions and discussions beyond the scope or purpose of the parable. The three parables of Luke 15 are told for one main reason, and a very essential reason—to encourage the emotion of repentance and forgiveness, especially within the family, and the joy that follows. What happens to the prodigal and his brother afterward, what kingdom the prodigal will enter, what the future of the prodigal and older brother will be, who will get what—all of this is not of any concern.

If we want a real life story to put these questions to rest, we need only read the story of Alma the Younger, who, though sinning grievously, still became the Lord's major instrument and the leader of His Church. There are none who were relegated to being only servants in the Lord's kingdom due to their former transgressions. There are only sons. There are only brothers, as Joseph assured his kneeling siblings at the death of Jacob when they feared vengeance would now be taken on them. They said, "Behold, we be thy servants." But Joseph said, "Am I in the place of God? . . . Fear ye not: I will nourish you, and your little ones. And he comforted them, and spake kindly unto them" (Genesis 50:18–19, 21). Brothers, not servants! Sons, not servants! Jesus told this deeply beloved parable to anchor that truth into our souls, both our younger- and our older-brother souls. We should have no problem understanding both points of view, but of course, the soul we want to possess is that of the father in the parable. Then coming near will see no hesitation. Then the words "This thy brother" will invoke only love and joy regardless of what he has done.

CHAPTER THREE

Seven Times in a Day

Forgiving Others

"And be ye kind one to another, tenderhearted, forgiving one
another, even as God for Christ's sake hath forgiven you."

EPHESIANS 4:32

"Moved with Compassion"

If we can learn to forgive and receive forgiveness within the boundaries of the family, it can become a template for the broader family of all God's children. Ironically, family forgiveness can often be the most difficult. Each type of forgiveness has its challenges and benefits. Within the family it can be easier to push away the negative memories by putting the positive ones in front until the negative become smaller and smaller on the soul's horizon. But the proximity of family life can also, if we choose to allow it, keep the actions ever present. With harms done outside the family, one may not have the opportunity to create positive moments to broaden the push-back separation with the ones that hurt us, because people may disappear from our lives. Family is always present, even if all verbal and visual contact is broken—they are still there. It is usually easier to walk away from those with whom we do not share the bonds of family ties.

Jesus gave the parable of the Prodigal Son to teach family

forgiveness; He taught other parables to teach forgiveness in the broader circle of our worlds—the Unmerciful Servant being, I believe, the main teaching. This is almost as well known as the Prodigal Son but may be worth another look. It was given in response to a statement made by Peter, who felt that forgiving one's brother seven times was a generous gift. But Jesus multiplied the number by seventy and told the story of two servants—one in debt to his lord and one in debt to his fellow servant. Their debts were vastly out of proportion to one another. One owed his lord ten thousand talents, an enormous sum; the other owed this same servant one hundred pence. Both pled for mercy and time to eliminate the debt. "Then the lord of that servant was *moved with compassion*, and loosed him, and forgave him the debt" (Matthew 18:27; emphasis added). This forgiveness was gracious indeed, for the servant had not asked for its removal but time to pay it. I think this is a most critical and curious detail and one we must not miss. The lord forgave more than was asked. He gave what was not asked! I think this is indicative of our Father in Heaven and His Son.

I recall once going to the Lord in embarrassment and shame for an action I should not have done to ask for forgiveness. How many times have I so asked? Before I could even petition, I received the distinct impression from the Spirit, "I understand. You need not ask. I have already forgiven." I suppose my very going to Him was a kind of asking, but the formality was waived and the forgiveness granted. I have tried not to take advantage of this kindness, but I have felt it more than once. We repeat often the Lord's words about prayer, "Ask, and it shall be given you" (Matthew 7:7). But this is not enough at times to describe what the Lord is willing to do for us. We might add, "It is often given to you before you ask and even when you fail to ask." Isaiah quotes the Lord as promising "that before they call, I will answer" (Isaiah 65:24).

Having had the weight of debt removed, the servant refuses to follow his lord's example regarding one who owed him the hundred pence. Instead he takes him by the throat and demands payment, eventually casting him into debtor's prison. Brought before his lord again he is asked, "I forgave thee all that debt, *because thou desiredst me*: shouldest not thou also have had *compassion* on thy fellowservant, even as I had *pity* on thee?" (Matthew 18:32–33; emphasis added). There are two key words we can focus on in this parable—*compassion* and *pity*. When Jesus applies the parable to all of us, He adds the admonition that we forgive "from [our] hearts" (Matthew 18:35). The Lord delights in forgiveness because, like the lord in the parable, He is always "moved with compassion." He is always filled with pity. These come from the core of His heart. Herein is a key to forgiving others—we pray for compassion, for pity, for the change of heart. Compassion is always outwardly centered. We can and should feel compassion for ourselves, and we will speak of forgiving the self in another chapter.

Part of our problem is to change from being driven by the head and the ego-dominated emotions to the heart, and by this I believe we are talking about the soul—that spiritual part of us that lifts us above the intellect and passions and is most sensitive to the attributes of God. On the level of the mind, justice has a greater claim. This is also true with the emotions. It seems reasonable to demand justice for my hurts, and the emotions fueled by pride may want the eye-for-an-eye approach to personal hurts, slights, deep pains, or humiliations. "I hurt, so I want you to hurt" also seems fair. There is a certain logic in it. Is this not just? We generally have no problems with justice—certainly not when it is directed to those who have hurt us. At its fullest, harshest manifestation, we want vengeance. Yet pity and compassion are what the Lord asks from us as a response. We can feel sorrow due to the injury. That is a legitimate emotion so long as it does not become self-pity. Jesus, remember, was a "man of sorrows" (Isaiah 53:3).

Room of Mirrors

What has sometimes helped me gain the necessary compassion and pity, apart from sincere prayer that the grace of God will help me acquire them, is to visualize myself in a room surrounded with mirrors. Everywhere I look I see myself. If I have been injured I see only my own pain. But each mirror is attached to the inside of the doors that have me confined in the small space of my own pain. We have difficulty forgiving at times because, as irrational as it sounds, our own ego's need for justice is greater than our desire for peace. We must set that need for immediate justice aside, trusting in the teaching of the Prophet Joseph Smith: "What can [these disasters] do? Nothing. All your losses will be made up to you in the resurrection, provided you continue faithful" (*Teachings of Presidents of the Church: Joseph Smith* [2007], 51).

I try to visualize the mirrored doors opening to the broader world or changing the mirrors to windows—to see others' pains, even the pain of the person who has done me the injury. This is the future vision that we talked of in the last chapter. That can be very difficult, if not impossible, especially in the rawness of an injury. Nevertheless, I need to feel something other than my own hurt or humiliation—to take myself out of myself somehow—to feel empathy. We can begin to sense the broader world and connect our own pain with the pain of others who share what we have experienced. Compassion is born. We are not alone in our pains. There is a broad world of humanity whom we understand and with whom we feel oneness.

I have tried to argue myself into forgiving or reason myself into forgiving or "doctrinalize" myself into forgiving, but usually this fails. I must *feel* my way into forgiving, and that usually isn't an act of the mind or rational thought. I enjoy hearing conference talks on repentance and forgiveness, but they often only increase my sense of guilt at having such a devil of a time trying to do it. Talking about forgiveness most often does not generate the empathy of forgiveness. It is when I open the doors, stop looking in the mirrors that reflect only my position, and see, know, and feel another's pain—any other person's pain—that the heart begins to soften somewhat and my own demand for justice, or that somebody pay a price equal to my own, diminishes. This is what happens in that interview discussed earlier, recorded in Moses 7, between Enoch and the Father. The Lord told Enoch "all the doings of the children of men; wherefore Enoch knew, and looked upon their wickedness, and their misery, and wept and stretched forth his arms, and his heart swelled wide as eternity; and his bowls yearned; and all eternity shook" (Moses 7:41). *Shook* in this context means to overflow, and the overflowing is one of compassion, pity, and love. Notice that Enoch looked on their wickedness. There was no attempt to lessen the extent of their crimes or the pain they had inflicted upon others, but their eventual suffering was also seen, and in that vision the compassion and pity were born. I feel God's pain, His compassion in this verse, and Enoch feels it also, which leads him to weep for those who will soon be swallowed up in the flood. That deluge is certainly in measure with justice, but I sense no satisfaction in either the Lord or Enoch that justice had been served in their destruction. There is only sorrow. We forgive on the level of the soul, not that of the mind or reason.

If we return to the Savior's parable, I think there may be a qualitative difference between compassion and pity, the two key words used by the lord when talking with the unmerciful servant. Compassion feels *with* the individual as if you were that person and brings catharsis; pity feels *for* them but leaves you still somewhat outside the other person. Compassion corresponds better with Jesus' words at the conclusion of His teaching that forgiveness comes from the heart. It has its highest percentage in the soul. Pity, perhaps, rests a little more in the mind, but it is at the soul level that we reach divine forgiveness. If we can't raise ourselves to the level of compassion, I believe the Lord will accept pity. It is a transitory step, but a step nonetheless, and it focuses us on the view outside the doors, not on the mirrors. That pity or compassion does not necessarily have to be for the offender at first. It can be directed outward to souls like our own—hurt souls. The necessary thing is to put something other than anger, humiliation, or resentment into the soul. We must move beyond the mirrors and the personal pain they reflect and will continue to reflect as long as we look into them.

Taking Account and Loosing the Debtor

I have also thought much about the words of Jesus early in the parable. "Therefore is the kingdom of heaven likened unto a certain king, which would *take account* of his servants" (Matthew 18:23; emphasis added). There will be an accounting in my own life and in your life. I will certainly be in the debtor's position, if not in ten-thousand-talent failings, in follies sufficient enough. I do not have any ten-thousand-talent sins, but I have ten thousand one-talent offenses, or, to reference another of the Savior's parables, I have a few hundred-pence transgressions that stand on the debit side of God's ledger. I will owe the Lord and others for so many debts accumulated in my life, many serious enough to cause me my own anguish. Yet I have one shining hope, and it is a significant one. I wish to say to my Father in Heaven at that time when He will "take account" of my life: "I acknowledge I owe thee greatly, Lord, *but no man owes me anything.* All debts have been forgiven. I have responded with compassion and pity. I have not demanded payment of my fellow servants. None remain in the prison of my heart." (The failure to forgive does turn the heart into a type of debtor's prison, does it not?) Just hearing my own voice say these words in the chambers of my soul can bring the grace of forgiveness into it. This may be the one thing the Lord wishes to hear. And I have a calm assurance that if we can reach that point of compassion and pity "from the heart," our own account-taking will be over.

I am impressed also in this parable by the words "the lord . . . loosed him" (Matthew 18:27). Of this I have thought a great deal. The question may not be only, "Have I forgiven?" but "Have I loosed the debtor?" This seems to imply a deeper level of forgiveness. Forgiveness usually means I "loose" myself from any hard feelings or demands of compensatory pain felt by those who have injured me. But must I "loose" the other person also? Perhaps—probably—if I can? To loose the other is to say or do whatever is necessary for that person to feel free also. This may require seven times seventy reassurances. It is a more difficult thing to accomplish, but it truly means I have moved the focus from myself and transferred it to my debtor. The mirrored doors are open to the view outside, or I have changed them into windows. I no longer look at the reflection of my injury but at how my compassion and pity can help the other forgive himself, if that is the particular problem, or even to loose the debtor from the self-deluding defenses he has set up that repels the desired forgiveness. Loosing others from their own defenses may be the greatest challenge we face. Jesus announced to His fellow villagers from Nazareth that He had come to preach deliverance to the captives. Who is captive to you and me, waiting for us to preach deliverance? It is not easy but shows the greatest compassion. We have arrived at one of the heights of forgiveness.

We need look no further than Joseph's words to his brothers when he first revealed his identity to them in Egypt. He knew their anguish and the pressing weight of guilt they carried. His own heart was free, but theirs were not, so he said to them: "Be not grieved, nor angry with yourselves . . . for God did send me before you to preserve life. . . . So now it was not you that sent me hither, but God" (Genesis 45:5, 8). These are gracious words offered to help remove the burden carried by his brothers. It is a perfect illustration of "loosing the debtor" as best one can.

Let me give you another more modern example. I use this

story because it combines the principle of coming near with that of loosing the debtor. I am familiar with a woman whose mother conceived her out of wedlock. This mother had problems in her own life and felt the addition of a child would overwhelm her, and she really didn't want the baby. She gave the infant girl away for adoption. Initially this gave the mother no pain. But as she grew older, her earlier actions troubled her greatly. Had she been selfish? What had happened to the little girl she bore and thought little of? Guilt began to grow as she reflected more and more. She began a search and in time found her daughter, now a mother of her own. A letter was written, and she waited for a response. The letter caused some deep soul-searching in my friend. She loved dearly the mother who raised her, but she felt compassion as she read of the turmoil in the woman who gave her birth. Though my friend felt no need to forgive a woman she had never known, she did have it in her power to loose her birth mother. An invitation to visit was offered and accepted. She established a relationship with her birth mother, allowing her into her life while assuring the mother whose love she had known from her first memory that no being could ever replace her in her life and love. This was a delicate situation, but one that offered healing. Here was a "coming-near" kindness, and in that coming near this lovely friend loosed a woman from the past with its painful emotions and guilt.

So often in the scriptural account we watch God loose the debtors by doing more than just forgiving them. He then graciously uses them for His own great work. Think, for instance, of Alma the Younger and the sons of Mosiah. We read that they "traveled throughout all the land . . . zealously striving to repair all the injuries which they had done. . . . Thus they were instruments in the hands of God in bringing many to the knowledge of the truth. . . . And how blessed are they!" (Mosiah 27:35–37). They knew the extent of that blessedness. Ammon, during his flight of joy at the goodness of God not only to him but also to the Lamanites, praised the Lord, the looser of his debts, with these words: "My joy is full, yea, my heart is brim with joy, and I will rejoice in my God. Yea, I know that I am nothing. . . . I cannot say the smallest part which I feel. Who could have supposed that our God would have been so merciful . . . ?" (Alma 26:11–12, 16–17). His joy and understanding of God's mercy were born of the knowledge of his own forgiveness, but he was equally astonished at the Lord's use of him in so great a work. Here was a loosing! Alma also was carried away with the gracious bounty of the Lord in allowing him to bring souls to forgiveness. In his hymn of adoration, so loved by the LDS people, Alma recorded, "I do not glory of myself, but I glory in that which the Lord hath commanded me; yea, and this is my glory, that perhaps I may be an instrument in the hands of God to bring some soul to repentance; and this is my joy" (Alma 29:9).

"Because Thou Desiredst Me"

I sense another beautiful truth in the conversations in the parable of the Unmerciful Servant. It is found in the Lord's reasons for releasing the debt. "I forgave thee all that debt, *because thou desiredst me*" (Matthew 18:32; emphasis added). We have already seen that the servant asked only for patience, for the time to pay the debt, not full release—the desire to be treated with mercy and leniency. Most of us would answer the question, "What do I need to do to be forgiven for my sins?" with a doctrinal, intellect-driven answer. "To be forgiven one must repent," we would say. I would never argue against this nor diminish its importance; I would simply point out that if the same question were asked of Jesus, He might respond in a different manner. Based on so many verses and instances in His life, I think He would answer that question two ways: "You need only ask. And be willing to forgive others." If we fall again, we ask again and forgive again—and on and on. The Lord forgave the ten-thousand-talent debt because "thou desiredst me." The request was enough. There was no formal procedure through what we often call the steps of repentance. The debtor simply desired. This is equally true of Alma the Younger during his "harrowing," when he pleaded for mercy. The desire was sufficient, and as is so often the case with our Father in Heaven, more than the desire was granted: in the parable it was full deliverance, not just time; in the story of Alma the Younger he was lifted into the very presence of God. In order to help members of the Church in our own time receive the peace of forgiveness, especially when transgressions are serious, various procedures and helps have been established that are motivated by love and have proved a blessing in many lives. I have seen these in operation and have been grateful to be a part of watching the Lord work His wonders in the lives of His children.

In another beautiful moment in the teachings of Jesus, the disciples were conversing with Him one day about offenses when He said, "Take heed to yourselves: If thy brother trespass against thee, rebuke him; and *if* he repent, forgive him. And if he trespass against thee *seven times in a day, and seven times in a day turn again to thee, saying, I repent; thou shalt forgive him*" (Luke 17:3–4;

emphasis added). Now one of the things that interests me about this verse is the two words "rebuke him." Unhappily, that is so very easy to do, and we might actually take delight in doing so, but if I am going to follow this aspect of the Savior's words I am under obligation to follow every part of His counsel in this verse, including the seven-times-in-a-day forgiveness. Perhaps by rebuke the Savior simply meant that if we have some kind of problem with the behavior of another we should talk about it rather than let it fester. The word from the Greek can also be translated "admonish, charge, or forbid." That may soften it somewhat.

I sometimes wish the *rebuke* part were not there and have wondered why it is. It seems to diminish the beauty of the counsel. Part of me wants this part to be an addition to the Savior's words by someone who felt it was a bit too much to ask of frail humanity otherwise. I forgive when *they* ask and I can *prompt* the asking. I am tempted to think these words are like those added in the Sermon on the Mount, "Whosoever is angry with his brother *without a cause* shall be in danger of the judgment" (Matthew 5:22; emphasis added). It sounds as though we *can* be angry with our brother, as long as there is justification. The puzzling thing about these words is they are not included in the Book of Mormon Sermon at Bountiful (see 3 Nephi 12:22). Nevertheless, "rebuke" is there, as well as that loophole "if," referring to my brother's repentance. So do I not need to forgive if there is no repentance? I would love to read it that way, as it lets me off the hook somewhat. I don't think there is a person alive who has not faced a situation where forgiveness is not asked for nor sorrow, shame, or apology shown or offered. However, almost always there is unease in the soul, a need to forgive regardless of what the other is doing. We would like the other to help us forgive by asking with sincerity and remorse, but the person may not. "My forgiving depends on you," I'd be tempted to think. "When you have sufficiently repented, and that includes all the steps, then and only then will the forgiveness be given." Yet I remember the father in the Prodigal Son running to embrace without knowing the son was coming home in humility and regret. It seems a bit more consistent with the Savior's teachings in other places that there is no "rebuke" and no "if." We just forgive, pretty much regardless of what the other person is doing, thinking, or feeling. (There are reasons for this that have to do with what hanging on to our injuries does to us.) This He instructed the early Saints to do in section 64 of the Doctrine and Covenants when some of the members were eager to point out the mistakes and sins of Joseph Smith. Some things never change. "Of you it is required to forgive all men" (D&C 64:10). The Lord acknowledges that Joseph did indeed have his own transgressions, but the Lord was continually forgiving him. If the Lord has forgiven, the issue should be closed and the same is expected of us; otherwise, we hold ourselves a higher judge than the Lord Himself. "There are those who have sought occasion against him without cause; nevertheless, he has sinned; but verily I say unto you, I, the Lord, forgive sins," especially, but not always necessarily, "who . . . ask forgiveness" (D&C 64:6-7). So let it go. "Let God judge between me and thee," the counsel continues, "and this ye shall do that God may be glorified—not because ye forgive not, having not compassion" (D&C 64:11, 13). Consequences may result from injury inflicted, justice may need to be satisfied, but in the heart there is forgiveness and compassion.

Section 98 of the Doctrine and Covenants was given in

response to the Missouri persecutions. Therein we also find an answer to our questions, "Do I need to forgive if there is no repentance, no apology, no regret or twinge of conscience coming from the offending person? What if the offenses are ongoing?" These can be challenging questions, especially if the offenses injure in deep ways. Some of this we will examine in a later chapter. The Lord repeats the need to forgive "until seventy times seven" the repenting enemy, "and shalt hold it no more as a testimony against" him (D&C 98:39–40). He then addresses our question directly. "If he trespass against thee and repent not the first time, nevertheless thou shalt forgive him. And if he trespass against thee the second time, and repent not, nevertheless thou shalt forgive him. And if he trespass against thee the third time, and repent not, thou shalt also forgive him" (D&C 98:41–43). If a fourth time occurs the Lord removes the command to forgive, counseling us to bring "these testimonies" before Him. It is now in His hands. However, if at this late date the offender repents, "Thou shalt forgive him with all thine heart" (D&C 98:44–45). These counsels are given by the Lord to cover everything from the individual problems we have with each other to international relations relating to war. This counsel can stop escalating division and hostility.

What does one do with the continuing transgression, either acknowledged or not? By this I mean the same offense repeated many times. Jesus told Peter to forgive seventy times seven, and that may mean for the same offense. This makes perfect sense to me, as there are things in my life with which I still fight. These are the continual weaknesses that cause us to repeat the same offense again and again. We are truly sorry for these things, but for whatever reason, our frailty, addiction, apathy, or despair over ever conquering the sin causes its repetition. Yet Jesus instructed His disciples to forgive seven times in the same day. Every time one asks for forgiveness, it should be given. Forgiveness is the one thing that we must never have a shortage of, must never run out of. I assume those seven single-day sins may be seven different ones, but they may also be the same one repeated. I used to tease my wife with this verse, saying I was allowed to make seven mistakes a day—to which she replied, "And you reach that limit often." She was right. It was a type of companion banter, but in reality that is what the Lord is asking us to do, particularly, as we have seen in an earlier chapter, if the person is a member of the family. I would also add a balancing thought. There are times when one must leave a relationship that is injurious. Forgiveness does not mean everything remains the same. It means the heart has been cleansed, even when continued association has ended. There are also times when reconciliation with the Church may be needed and helpful, and in His far-sighted vision the Lord has placed into operation the means to accomplish this under loving and watchful care and guidance.

I anticipate that the Savior never asked of us what He Himself would not do. So we can be assured that each time we go to Him with the same repeated offense in real sorrow He will forgive, just as He will forgive seven different weaknesses occurring on the same day. He might forgive us even if we don't have real sorrow, knowing that ultimately we will, and so He forgives in anticipation of that future remorse. It is not hard for me to believe this, as I have done it on a much smaller scale with the offenses of my own children. In other words, His compassion, pity, and love are tireless and long-suffering, and so must ours be, as hard as it is sometimes to live it. As in all things, the very desire to follow His example and counsels and the tiniest of our efforts will be accepted and encouraged. Do not the Psalms testify, "Like as a father pitieth his children, so the Lord pitieth them that fear [reverence] him. For he knoweth our frame; he remembereth that we are dust" (Psalm 103:13-14).

"Nothing to Pay"

There is another beautiful story of forgiveness complete with its own parable recorded in the Gospel of Luke. Luke was the most tender of all Gospel writers. Jesus is eating at the home of one Simon, a Pharisee, when a woman enters weeping. She washes His feet with tears, dries them with her hair, and then anoints His feet with ointment. All this is done as silence prevails in the room. Simon assumes that Jesus cannot be a prophet or He would know what manner of woman was touching Him. This brings forth from the Savior a parable similar to the Unmerciful Servant in that it contains two debtors. One owes five hundred pence and the other fifty. "And when they had *nothing to pay*," the Savior continued, "he *frankly* forgave them both. . . . Which of them will love him most?" (Luke 7:42; emphasis added). Once again, part of the power of this episode in the life of the Savior is in its ability to impart to us as reading witnesses the feeling of forgiveness. As we have already seen, this is the primary manner the scriptures help us learn to forgive and be forgiven. I never read this story without being deeply moved by both the woman and the Savior. She was doing all she could. I love two things in particular about this parable. First, the word "frankly"—it is so clean, uncluttered, and unhindered. Forgiveness is flowing freely. We see it again in the Book of Mormon when Nephi is tied up by his brothers while returning with Ishmael's family and he "frankly" forgives them (see 1 Nephi 7:21). The second is the phrase "nothing to pay." This does not mean "I don't owe you anything," which can be the attitude of some, but "I don't have anything to remove your hurt. If I could, I would do so." The phrase "nothing to pay" generates empathy within us. There is a kind of hopelessness about the two debtors that softens the heart. Sometimes our actions or those of others that hurt us leave us or them with nothing to pay. Even if one desired to pay, there is nothing that can be done to make amends or to make things better. There are only tears such as the woman gave. They can't heal the hurt. In our human weakness we may want the offending person to pay—pay with guilt, sorrow, shame, embarrassment, tears, and ointment, or we may frankly forgive. Many times I have said to a child, friend, or Laurie, "I have nothing to pay. I wish I had not brought this upon you, but I can't move the sundial shadow backward. I have nothing to pay." When one has nothing to pay, it is then the opportunity of the forgiving person to loose the debtor, inasmuch as it is in his or her power to do so. To quote Shakespeare's King Lear, in that great play of forgiveness—"Upon such sacrifices, my Cordelia, the gods themselves throw incense" (*King Lear*, Act V, scene III, lines 20-21).

Seeing the Woman

After relating the parable, Jesus turned to Simon and said something that also never fails to create a feeling of forgiveness within me. "And he turned to the woman, and said unto Simon, *Seest thou this woman?*" (Luke 7:44; emphasis added). He was looking at her as He posed this question, because He turned toward her. There may be times in all of our lives when we are expected to forgive someone who has injured us or one we love, and the Savior asks us the same question. "Seest thou this woman? Or this man? Or this child? Or this spouse? Or this leader?" It can be so very hard to see the person and not our own pain, but the only way to really gain release from that pain is to take our eyes off our own hurt and try to see as Jesus did on this occasion. We can so easily be diverted from the person to our pain. We choose the inner view instead of the outer one. I know, for I have done it often enough. But how can we see the person without constantly being reminded of the pain that person caused us? In that we pray fervently for the grace of God. Part of the grace He gives us is in helping the hurt create in us compassion for others who may be suffering in kind. We may not be looking at the offender, but we are not looking at ourselves, either. The mirrors are down. It provides a more neutral platform to stand upon until we can climb higher and let the compassion include the one who hurt us. We learn to see past the pain and with God's help respond to an unjust and at times uncaring world with love, mercy, and kindness. We learn to take our own suffering and injury and allow it to change us, to lift us higher than the despair or anger. We learn to be part of the solution to the world's pain, and that solution is love and mercy. Ironic as it seems, pain can be very influential in the creation of love. We learn we are stronger than anything life can throw at us, for compassion, kindness, and mercy are stronger than transgression, anguish, and heartache. That is an eternal truth.

At times I try to fight deep feelings with reason—the heart's injuries with the mind's conversations. I am an intellect-oriented person. It usually does not work. I can't argue myself into forgiveness. A better strategy is to fight feelings with more powerful feelings. Bitterness, resentment, humiliation, sorrow, anger, and hate are all very strong emotions, perhaps too strong for the mind, especially when they are new, but I firmly believe that the positive emotions generate greater depth. We must have faith that empathy, compassion, mercy, long-suffering, and love are more than equal to the task of diminishing if not removing the emotions of injury. We can also feel gratitude for the Lord's compensatory graces in our life. We turn the mirrors of our egos, which see only our pain, into windows that look on others' pain or God's goodness. We use the wounding to enliven our ability to recognize, understand, and identify with humanity's pain. We are not alone in our temptations or suffering. Paul told the Corinthians that there was no experience of life that was not common to a broad spectrum of people. "There hath no temptation taken you but such as is common to man," he wrote (1 Corinthians 10:13). By *temptation* he meant more than sin, but a broad swath of life's experiences. We do recognize that the temptation to withhold forgiveness is indeed a temptation. The Lord told the early Saints of he who doesn't forgive, "there remaineth in him the greater sin" (D&C 64:9) That is hard doctrine when you hurt. I suppose one of the reasons for this is the continuing and growing nature of bitterness and resentment. Like a plant it draws strength from the soil of the heart's negativity and matures. There is hope, however, in the knowledge that bitterness and resentment and self-pity cannot dwell in the same heart at the same time with compassion, mercy, kindness, empathy, and gratitude. I don't need to feel these emotions for the person who wounded me, at least not at first, for as much as we desire to, it may not be possible right away, but I can certainly feel those positive emotions for others in similar circumstances and push away the darkness with the light of love.

This life is an educative process. God is trying to make us into beings like Himself, and He can take every experience and shape us with it if we allow Him, but He can't do this if we continue to feel sorry for ourselves or bitter or want to tell other people how much they injured us. Our eyes are still looking in the ego's mirrors; they are not "seeing the woman." They are not seeing the broader world of humanity. Now I will grant that it may be easier for Jesus to forgive because the woman's sins were not against Him specifically, but what about the husband—if there was one, if that was her sin? We are not told the specifics, but we are told that her sins were "many" (Luke 7:47). If there wasn't a hurt spouse in this case there surely was in the case of the woman brought to Jesus on the temple mount, for we read that she was taken in the very act of adultery. Yet in this story also we are invited by the actions of Jesus to focus on the person and on the person only. "When Jesus had lifted up himself, and *saw none but the woman*" (John 8:10; emphasis added). I love those words dearly. I want to reach a point in my life where I see none but the woman and in that seeing learn to forgive as did our Master. So let us release our need to wound others because we are wounded. Let us let go of the need to let others know how much we suffer. In looking in the mirrors we will only hurt ourselves. Let the mirrors become windows to the world outside ourselves. The mirrors will trap you in the pains of the past; through the windows you can see the sunlight of the future. Out of the ashes of evil and injustice arises the phoenix of goodness and compassion, if we so choose.

Zeniff also gives us a new way of "seeing the woman," which may be difficult when we can still feel the wounds of past injuries. While leading a spying mission in Lamanite lands with the intention to "destroy them," Zeniff states, "When *I saw that which was good among them* I was desirous that they should not be destroyed" (Mosiah 9:1; emphasis added). He wishes then to make a treaty and live in peace. How beautifully and quickly the old hates and injuries melt away by simply looking for something good among the enemy. This represents a powerful way of "seeing the woman." We may hesitate to look for such qualities because we don't want to give up the negative feelings, and seeing goodwill always challenge those feelings, but Zeniff's view never fails to lessen anger and resentment while fostering goodwill and acceptance. I believe this vision of others is what Paul meant when he stated that charity "thinketh no evil; rejoiceth not in iniquity, but rejoiceth in the truth" (1 Corinthians 13:5-6). If we are not careful we may be glad in thinking of the vices of others and hesitant to hear anything good about them. It has sobered me more than once to remember who delights in the negative characteristics of people. I would read that last statement of Paul, as it applies to forgiveness, as meaning that one with charity rejoices in the knowledge of the goodness still to be found in the enemy, as Zeniff found it.

Susannah Cibber

I related earlier that I gather forgiveness stories. One of my favorites involves an eighteenth-century actress named Susannah Cibber. I tell the story every year in Dublin, where the *Messiah* was first performed in April 1742. Susannah is intricately tied to that first performance of Handel's masterpiece, which provides a wonderful setting for forgiveness, as it is the single most loved piece of music closely associated with the Savior of all time. Susannah acted and sang. Her voice was not particularly strong, but she put such sincere feeling into everything she did that audiences were entranced and moved by her singing. It was said of Susannah that she penetrated the heart, not the ear, by connecting to the words or role she played. Handel discovered her, and though he was not generally patient with singers, he took particular pains to work with Susannah. She could not read music. She was born Susannah Arne, marrying Theophilus Cibber under intense pressure from her ambitious brother and father, who thought they could profit from the marriage. Theophilus was an actor and manager of a well-known theater in London on Drury Lane. He was a hard-drinking, womanizing, gambling man who had already brought his first wife to the grave. He promptly began to profit from his new wife, going so far as to take all of Susannah's jewelry and costumes in a drunken rage to help cover his debts. Susannah faced the death of two infants, and Theophilus gave her a venereal disease. He began to pressure Susannah into receiving the attentions and gifts of male callers who hung around the theater. Susannah refused, knowing what they would ultimately want. When Theophilus brought the son of a wealthy squire named William Sloper to Susannah, the outcome was not what he fully anticipated. Happy to encourage the affair as long as he got money, Theophilus was distressed to learn that the gentle nature of William and the need for love and caring from Susannah produced first a sincere and deep affection and eventually love. Susannah asked for a divorce and then ran away with William when it was refused. A daughter was born, and Theophilus sued the Slopers for a fortune on the charge of "Criminal Conversation." It was the case of the century, full of the sensationalism so loved by the press and public. Theophilus won, but the court awarded him the tiniest sum for injury it could, knowing his nature. It was a victory in some ways for the Sloper family, but in order to win, the lawyer had to decimate Susannah's character, completely destroying her reputation. A salacious book was written based on the famous trial, which further ridiculed and shamed her, portraying Susannah as a seductress. Her career was over. William and Susannah moved into the country to raise their daughter.

At this time, Handel's own success in London was waning. From a friend named Charles Jennens he received the scripture compilation that would inspire him to write in a very short time the music to the *Messiah*. Discouraged with the dwindling London audiences, Handel accepted an invitation to perform a season in Dublin, bringing the new oratorio with him. This same year a close friend of Susannah, James Quin, invited her to perform with him in Dublin, including in several Shakespearean plays. Thus the famous composer and the shamed singer came together again for music history. Handel gave Susannah the longest aria in the *Messiah*, written for her range and based on Isaiah's words in two chapters. "He [was] despised and rejected of men; a man of sorrows, and acquainted with grief. [He] gave [his] back to the smiters, and [his] cheeks to them that plucked off the hair: [he] hid not [his] face from shame and spitting" (see Isaiah 53:3; 50:6). It is the one moment in the oratorio that most demands intense emotion, and Susannah's voice and experiences combined with powerful effect. The first performance in Dublin was done for charity at the Easter season. On the afternoon of April 13th, 1742, Susannah stood up and sang words and music that she could comprehend and appreciate in a personal way. She sang as if her own soul was connected to that of her Savior, aware in a profound manner of what Jesus had suffered and what He could forgive. In the audience that afternoon was Dr. Patrick Delaney, the chancellor of St. Patrick's Cathedral, a respected clergyman and friend to Jonathan Swift. Having recently lost his wife, his emotions and feelings were sensitive and tender. Moved deeply by Susannah, he rose from his seat as she concluded her aria and called out to her on the stage, his voice filling the music hall. "Woman, for this be all thy sins forgiven thee!" It was a turning point for Susannah.

"Seest thou this woman?" Jesus had once asked the Pharisee, Simon. Patrick Delaney saw the woman—not her sins, not her shame, not the scandal. Forgiveness truly is a beautiful thing—life-changing and enriching. Susannah returned to the London stage, singing in the first performance of the *Messiah* there as well as in many of Handel's other compositions. In time her career was resurrected as she continued to sing and act, becoming one of the greatest actresses to perform on the London stage. When he died, Handel was buried in Westminster Abbey in Poet's Corner, one of the most singular honors bestowed by the British people. Susannah rests not far from him.

"She Loved Much"

The story related in Luke chapter 7 ends in love. Jesus tells Simon, "I say unto thee, Her sins, which are many, are forgiven; *for she loved much*" (Luke 7:47; emphasis added). Our love increases when we are on the receiving end of forgiveness and the person on the other end does not demand a payment that we cannot give—when we have "nothing to pay." The recognition of that truth helps us when we are on the forgiving end. As I alluded to earlier, when I was an infant, my father, for weaknesses within his own life, left our family. A civil divorce and cancellation of sealing eventually followed, and I rarely saw my father for years. He did not exhibit much of a desire to have anything to do with his children. I later found out this was due to fear rather than apathy. At one point in my life I felt strongly motivated to engage in my father's life and try to create a relationship with him. At that time I had no concept of the principles of "loosing another," "coming near," "seeing the woman," or "nothing to pay"; I just felt pushed by the Spirit. In this effort my sisters and I were successful, and in time, as mentioned earlier, he returned to full activity in the Church and shared in the later part of his life family inclusion with his children and grandchildren. Part of my empathy for my father and a source of great healing was the knowledge, born out of "seeing" him, that he knew he had nothing to pay for the wasted years when he could have played a greater role in our lives. His choices were truly tragic. I gained a great deal of compassion interacting with my father. He has now passed away, but the thought that he really had nothing to pay continues to fill me with kindness and empathy and the hope that he will receive every mercy God can extend. In truth I would say to the Lord, "You don't need to extend forgiving mercy to my father, because in my mind and heart there is no transgression—nothing to forgive." When we try to live the principles as Jesus taught them, we will discover how very powerful love can be for both parties.

A totally forgiving life may not be possible for us. We are not Jesus. But we can keep anger, resentment, pain, and bitterness at a distance. Time helps us if we don't let the old wounds remain sore and unhealed. Most of all we will put compassion, love, understanding, and empathy for our fellow man who suffers just as we do between us and the past until we can all say, "Lord, no man owes me anything." This will be a lifelong pursuit. Did not Jesus encourage us to include forgiveness in every prayer when He offered what we call the Lord's Prayer? Along with asking for our daily bread, we beseech Him to "forgive us our debts, as we forgive our debtors. And lead us not into temptation, but deliver us from evil" (Matthew 6:12-13). This we need as much as bread, and as often. Jesus taught us to pray, "Help us, Lord, not to hurt others by our own yielding; and deliver us from the pain others may put upon us. Touch the love in our souls and draw out of them the forgiving heart. Help us to remember that our own wounds can unite us with others who also have been wounded"—which includes just about all of humanity!

CHAPTER FOUR

Bruised Reeds

Receiving Divine Forgiveness

*"As often as my people repent will I forgive
them their trespasses against me."*

MOSIAH 26:30

The God Who Winks

There are many reasons why Jesus came to earth, and our word *Atonement* has come to embody them all, but I think, if I had to be specific, I would say that the essence of His life centered on forgiveness. In the great hymn of the Restoration, Joseph Smith caught that spirit when he wrote, "Now, what do we hear in the gospel which we have received? A voice of gladness! A voice of mercy from heaven" (D&C 128:19). The Savior is the incarnation, the personification, the grand architect of forgiveness and mercy. It is inherent in almost every act of His life. It is the one single most significant quality of the Father that Jesus came to teach us with His words and show us by His example. Indeed, the most beautiful words He spoke during those last agonizing hours of His life are, "Father, forgive them; for they know not what they do" (Luke 23:34). Whenever I feel the difficulty of forgiving in my own life, I read those words and the feeling of forgiveness moves into my soul.

I believe it is more than critical that we reach a certainty of knowledge of how very easy it is for Him to forgive. He delights in forgiveness. He is mercy and He is love. I wish this were true of you and me, but in our humanity we can find it daunting. Perhaps because we struggle with this grace we may wonder about God and our relationship with Him. "My thoughts are not your thoughts, neither are your ways my ways, saith the Lord" (Isaiah 55:8). I must sometimes remind myself that God simply does not view things the way I do. Mankind has far too often created God in *their* image, justifying even the most terrible of acts. Unfortunately, religion can be very effective in shutting the mind down from thinking and the heart from feeling. I quote the above words from Isaiah because the verse immediately preceding them and contained in the same paragraph assures us that if the wicked "forsake his way, and the unrighteous man his thoughts: and . . . return unto the Lord, . . . he will have mercy upon him; and . . . will abundantly pardon" (Isaiah 55:7). His ways and His thoughts are merciful thoughts and forgiving ways, though humanity's ways may not be.

Just how abundantly is "abundantly"? Literally hundreds of scriptures come to mind. I think of Paul's words to the citizens of Athens when he was teaching them from Mars Hill. He had wandered through the Agora, which was filled with idols and temples to pagan gods who had been worshipped for centuries. Here was violation of the first two of the Ten Commandments. Yet it was all so easily waved aside with one word in Paul's address. "And the times of this ignorance God *winked* at" (Acts 17:30; emphasis added). I love that word! God winked at it all! I can't tell you how comforting it is to know that we worship a "winking God." In the footnote we learn that in the Greek, the word means to overlook or disregard. Vine, who wrote a dictionary of all New Testament words from the Greek, describes it this way: "God bore with them without interposing by way of punishment" (*Expository Dictionary of New Testament Words* [Barbour & Company, Inc., 1940], 220).

Paul would know about a God who winked, for this same God had forgiven him while he was in a state of hostility and intolerance while traveling on the road to Damascus. Paul is described as "breathing out threatenings and slaughter," something, unfortunately, that has happened too often within religion. He had not asked the Lord to intervene in his life. Yet he was called by a voice of gentleness and meekness, which simply and with love asked him a single question: "Saul, Saul, why persecutest thou me?" (Acts 9:1, 4). Here was winking. That voice of mildness changed everything. Paul would speak of it for the rest of his life, as it was the defining moment in his mortal journey—a moment of forgiveness. It made Paul what he was, and it would be Paul, perhaps more than any other man, that spread Christianity and thus assured its continuation. In his epistle to Timothy, Paul tried to explain why he felt God had shown him this mercy: "Jesus came into the world to save sinners; of whom I am chief. Howbeit for this cause I obtained mercy, that in me first Jesus Christ might shew forth all longsuffering, for a pattern to them which should hereafter believe on him to life everlasting" (1 Timothy 1:15–16). Paul earlier told Timothy, "The grace of our Lord was *exceeding abundant with . . . love* which is in Christ Jesus" (1 Timothy 1:14; emphasis added). There is that word "abundant" again.

The scriptures deal in extreme stories that sit somewhat outside of the norms of life. They are constructed this way for a reason. Everything less is thereby covered. If God can forgive Paul, He can forgive you and me. "I am the example," Paul is saying, "of the abundant love of the Savior." Alma the Younger and the sons of Mosiah exemplify this same truth in the Book of Mormon. Paul told the Saints in Ephesus that God "is *rich in mercy*, for his *great love* wherewith he loved us." We cannot know, Paul continued, "the *breadth, and length, and depth, and height*," of "the love of Christ, which *passeth knowledge*" (Ephesians 2:4; 3:18–19; emphasis added). It has no boundaries, as Enoch testified when his own "heart swelled wide as eternity." Jesus would later take that image and describe Himself as "the Rock of Heaven, which is broad as eternity" (Moses 7:41, 53). This love, this richness of mercy, pity, and compassion, enables Him "to do *exceeding abundantly* above all that we ask or think," for the "love of Christ . . . passeth knowledge" (Ephesians 3:19–20; emphasis added). Paul himself was just one of so many examples.

"How Oft Will I Gather You"

Lest we doubt this with the pressing of our own guilt, the Lord provided other stories to bear home the point, particularly in the Book of Mormon. Ammon, speaking in behalf of himself and his brothers, said, "Who can say too much of his great power, and of his mercy. . . . Behold, we went forth even in wrath, with mighty threatenings to destroy his church [just like Paul]. Oh then, why did he not consign us to an awful destruction, yea, why did he not let the sword of his justice fall upon us, and doom us to eternal despair?. . . . He did not exercise his justice upon us, but in his great mercy hath brought us over that everlasting gulf of . . . misery" (Alma 26:18-20). Alma the Younger would bear a similar testimony to the forgiving power of the Father and Son. When "racked" and "harrowed" by the memories of his past life, Alma wished for extinction. "The very thought of coming into the presence of my God did rack my soul with inexpressible horror. Oh, thought I, *that I could be banished and become extinct both soul and body*, that I might not be brought to stand in the presence of my God" (Alma 36:14-15; emphasis added). That is hiding far beyond the fig leafs of Eden. In some respects we might say it is the ultimate of all fig-leaf aprons. Yet in the moment of a prayer, in the reaching of his soul, Alma cried, "O Jesus, thou Son of God, have mercy on me." The compassion flowed immediately, the balm of forgiveness healing even in the utterance of the prayer. "I could remember my pains no more; yea, I was harrowed up by the memory of my sins no more" (Alma 36:18-19). Joy replaces fear, and in vision Alma sees the throne of the Father, "Yea, and my soul did long to be there" (Alma 36:22). That is quite a shift! We swing from horror of God to longing for Him in an instant. Yes, God's ways are not our ways, but we will try to emulate Him. At least we can believe Him. I think it is also indicative of our Father in Heaven and His Son that between Paul and Alma, one asked for mercy and the other did not, but both received it. It didn't seem to matter; the compassion and forgiving was forthcoming nonetheless.

The Book of Mormon rebounds with similar if not so dramatic examples. We enter Nephi's heart in the hymn he wrote found in 2 Nephi chapter 4, where he cried out, "I am encompassed about, because of the temptations and the sins which do so easily beset me . . . *nevertheless, I know in whom I have trusted*" (2 Nephi 4:18–19; emphasis added). There is Enos praying in the woods and hearing the voice of God in his mind say, "Enos, thy sins are forgiven thee, and thou shalt be blessed" (Enos 1:5). I love the second part of that forgiving—not just the removal of the guilt, but the addition of a blessing. It is God's way. He blesses so often in anticipation. There are King Benjamin's people, who cry out for cleansing and are immediately answered when "the Spirit of the Lord came upon them, and they were filled with joy, having received a remission of their sins" (Mosiah 4:3). Forgiveness is simply the theme of the Book of Mormon; without even looking you will find it everywhere. Zeezrom, with "his mind . . . exceedingly sore because of his iniquities" (Alma 15:5) was merely asked if he believed in the Savior when he received healing peace. Lamoni cried, "O Lord, have mercy; according to thy abundant mercy . . . upon me, and my people" (Alma 18:41). His queen echoed his prayer later, "saying: O blessed Jesus . . . O blessed God, have mercy on this people" (Alma 19:29). Alma's son Corianton, having sinned during his mission among the Zoramites, causing it to largely fail, was still told by his father, "O my son, ye are called of God to preach the word unto this people. And now, my son, go thy way, declare the word with truth and soberness, that thou mayest bring souls unto repentance, that the great plan of mercy may have claim upon them" (Alma 42:31). Even the Lamanites who were preparing to kill the brothers Nephi and Lehi in prison cried out for mercy when covered by the dark mist. Then "they were encircled about, yea every soul, by a pillar of fire. . . . And they were filled with that joy which is unspeakable and full of glory." They then heard the voice of God whispering, "Peace, peace be unto you, because of your faith in my Well Beloved" (Helaman 5:43-44, 47). All these examples of God's forgiving love are brought to a climax in Third Nephi, when the voice of Jesus speaks through the darkness of destruction the beautiful, soothing, and inviting words, "How oft *have* I gathered you as a hen gathereth her chickens under her wings, and have nourished you. . . . How oft *will* I gather you as a hen gathereth her chickens under her wings, if ye will repent and return unto me with full purpose of heart" (3 Nephi 10:4-6; emphasis added).

"I Will; Be Thou Clean"

When we read these many accounts, as we have seen so often, they fill us with the spirit of forgiveness, and in the grace of that spirit we too can forgive and believe that we can be forgiven. We may not be able to hold that forgiveness in the heart continually, but we have felt it for a moment, and that moment can expand in time. *Everyone who asks forgiveness in the Book of Mormon receives it, and they receive it immediately!* It is the one great constant in that most constant of books. As a further witness to its testimony of forgiveness, even a casual reading of the Doctrine and Covenants will reveal a God who is persistently and frequently forgiving. You will find it in section after section. I think often of Martin Harris, who was called in section 3 and 10 "a wicked man" (D&C 3:12; 10:7) for his role in the loss of the 116 pages of Book of Mormon manuscript, yet was still chosen shortly thereafter in section 17 as one of the Three Witnesses. This was more than mere forgiveness; herein God was loosing Martin's debt. The swing from wicked man to witness is great, but easily within the scope of a God who winks.

"Ye are little children," the Lord told the early Saints, "and ye cannot bear all things now; nevertheless, be of good cheer, for I will lead you along. The kingdom is yours and the blessings thereof are yours" (D&C 78:17-18). "Listen to him who is the advocate with the Father, who is pleading your cause before him—saying . . . Father, spare these my brethren that believe on my name, that they may come unto me and have everlasting life" (D&C 45:3-5).

I would point out also that in so many of these examples not only is forgiveness granted, but the individuals rise to positions of trust and usefulness in God's kingdom. There is no blacklist in heaven. Nothing remains "on the record." No future opportunities or blessings are forfeited forever or even during mortality. I know a man whom I love deeply who won't return to activity because he believes his past sins will remain a permanent stain on his Church records and that he can never serve in a position of trust. The sons of Mosiah became the key to mass Lamanite conversion, the most effective of all scriptural missionaries, and Alma headed not only the nation but the Church as well. The Lamanites in the prison with Nephi and Lehi spread throughout the land and brought an end to over five hundred years of animosity between Nephite and Lamanite, uniting the two peoples. Isaiah taught this totality of cleansing and forgiveness with one of the most quoted verses on forgiveness: "Come now, and *let us reason together*, saith the Lord: though your sins be as scarlet, they shall be as white as snow; though they be red like crimson, they shall be as wool" (Isaiah 1:18; emphasis added). I have said many times to myself and others, and have written, "There are no pink people in the Lord's kingdom." Though I believe strongly that forgiveness, whether receiving it ourselves or extending it to others, is not an act of the mind, but of the soul, it is *reasonable* to believe that God can turn the crimson life into the snow life. It is so because of the type of a God He is—the winking God, the God of Paul and Alma, of Enos and Lamoni—the God who forgives beyond the breadth, length, depth, and height of our understanding, the God who forgives above all we can ask or think, the broad-as-eternity God. Hence we read that first word of invitation—the simple single word—"come."

So many of the miracles Jesus performed for individuals were done to teach us what He wanted and would do for us all on the spiritual level. He opened the eyes of the blind; He would open our eyes to see truth. He blessed the deaf with hearing as He would give us ears to hear the words of His Father. He fed the five thousand as He would feed and nourish us with truth and the assurance there are always twelve baskets of enlightenment to receive when we have feasted and been filled. The list goes on and on. Perhaps my favorite of all healings was one of the most simple—that of a leper. I can never read it without tears. The leper's cry is your cry and my cry, and I utter it almost every day of my life. "And there came a leper to him, beseeching him, and kneeling down to him, and saying unto him, *If thou wilt, thou canst make me clean. And Jesus, moved with compassion, put forth his hand, and* touched him, and saith unto him, *I will; be thou clean.*" I too have come before my Lord in the uncleanness of my own spiritual leprosy (have not we all?), beseeching and kneeling and crying, "Lord, if thou wilt, thou canst make me clean." Always, in every circumstance, I hear Him say, "I will; be thou clean." The immediacy of that cleansing is displayed here also, for we read, "And as soon as he had spoken, *immediately* the leprosy departed from him, and he was cleansed" (Mark 1:40-42; emphasis added). I can't help but notice that this cleansing is one of the first miracles Mark relates in his Gospel—in the very first chapter.

Paul was so convinced of the Savior's mercy that he had to plead in his epistle to the Romans that the Saints not take advantage or abuse the Lord's kindness, knowing it was so easily bestowed. "I can always repent," someone might say. Ironically—emphatically—this is true, and Paul was concerned some might not avoid sin, assured that forgiveness would always come. "Despisest thou the riches of his goodness and forbearance and longsuffering;" he asked, "not knowing that the goodness of God leadeth thee to repentance?" (Romans 2:4). "His forgiving nature is a perpetual invitation to come and be cleansed," Paul is saying, "That is its purpose. Please don't impose on it." To the Hebrews he wrote: "We have not an high priest which cannot be *touched with the feeling of our infirmities;* but was in all points tempted like as we are, yet without sin. Let us therefore *come boldly* unto the throne of grace, that we may obtain mercy, and find grace to help in time of need" (Hebrews 4:15-16; emphasis added).

"A Bruised Reed Shall He Not Break"

Sin is a spiritual bruising. It can make us tender. We have all been bruised, and, to our regret, we have also bruised others. Like Alma, we may fear contact with God. Experience seems to teach us that one of the first things people cease to do when faced with their own partaking of forbidden fruits is to pray. But that is exactly what we need to do and, as Paul teaches, to do with boldness. There are so many very lovely, gentle, and tender moonlight truths in Isaiah. Like David, he knew the heart of the Shepherd-God he worshipped. "He shall not cry, nor lift up, nor cause his voice to be heard in the street," he wrote of God. We do not worship a railing God. He is not harsh. He is not a rebuking Father. "Doubtless thou art our father . . . our redeemer," Isaiah pleaded. "Be not wroth very sore . . . behold, see, we beseech thee, we are all thy people" (Isaiah 42:2; 63:16; 64:9). Our Father will not censure, not scold, when we come to Him with our tender souls bruised by sin. "A bruised reed shall he not break, and the smoking flax shall he not quench," Isaiah said (Isaiah 42:3). What a beautiful image. It catches what we may feel sometimes. Reeds are hollow and stand up only if the cylinder remains whole, but if you bruise or pinch the reed it no longer stands straight. Life can bruise, and in the bruising the small fires of faith burning in the heart may dwindle into smoking flax, but the Lord is so gentle in His dealing with us that though we are bruised He will not cry nor lift up the voice in condemnation. "Neither do I condemn thee," He told the woman taken in adultery without her having said any other words to Him than, "No man, Lord," in response to His question. Then: "Go, and sin no more" (John 8:11). He expressed the same kind mercy to the woman in Simon's house whose tears washed His feet. "Thy faith hath saved thee; go in peace" (Luke 7:50). They were bruised reeds; they were smoking flax. He will fan the fires of faith within the smoking flax of our hearts back into brightness. He does not quench nor break anyone. If this is true of those who inflict injuries on others, how much more confidence can we have that He will heal the bruised reeds who have suffered through the sins and weaknesses of others?

What does God want in return for His forgiveness? Certainly a forgiving heart toward others; of this we have many witnesses. But in addition, perhaps, the woman in Simon's house teaches best what we offer our winking God as her actions answered Jesus' question to Simon, "Which of them will love him most?" So it is love God desires in return. And she does love! "Wherefore I say unto thee, Her sins, which are many, are forgiven; for she loved much" (Luke 7:42, 47). There is such poignancy in a God who asks of us love, perhaps even a touch of vulnerability. To Enoch, who saw Him weeping, the Father said: "Unto thy brethren have I said, and also given commandment, that they should . . . choose me, their Father; but behold, they are without affection" (Moses 7:33). If one can feel for God empathy, I feel it here. We sense that same empathy in the writings of Isaiah, where God pleads with His people with equal poignancy. He desires obedience, of course, but His motivation is entirely for our own happiness. Some may feel that obedience is what God wants most of all, but He is a father embodying all that is most dear about a father. Obedience without love is a type of tyranny, and God is not oppressive. This is a God who loves and loves deeply, and like all of us He desires love in return. Surely in this we can understand the heart of God as well as Christ.

"Thou hast not called upon me, O Jacob," we read the Lord saying in Isaiah, "thou hast been weary of me, O Israel. Thou hast not brought me the small cattle of thy burnt offerings; neither hast thou honoured me with thy sacrifices. . . . Thou hast brought me no sweet cane . . . but thou hast . . . wearied me with thine iniquities" (Isaiah 43:22–24). What the Lord wanted was the heart of the people, and though the sacrifices He had asked of them were not difficult, nor had He "wearied" them with His commandments, yet their devotion was shallow. Instead of sacrifice, incense, prayer, or worship they brought to His altars their sins. Does He accept this "offering"? Yes! "I, even I, am he that blotteth out thy transgressions for mine own sake, and will not remember thy sins" (Isaiah 43:25). We love the Lord and try our very best to show that love. You and I bring Him our devotions, our prayers, our service, our gratitude, but we also bring to Him our sins, asking Him to take them also. And He does! In return for taking them and then not remembering them, He asks of us that we do remember something. "Put me in remembrance: let us plead together" (Isaiah 43:26). He has even given us an ordinance *that we might remember that He does not remember.* I think of that when I take the sacrament. We stand *with* our Savior, not before Him. When I hear those lovely words in both sacrament prayers, "always remember him," there is much to reflect upon, but one thing fills me with the spirit of forgiveness, and that is the knowledge that *He does not remember.* That is what you and I must "always remember" and never forget. Each time we partake of the sacrament we can hear His voice saying, "Always remember that I am the Great Forgetter." Then we will love Him and we will plead with Him, as He invites us to do in Isaiah, in remembrance of the sublime forgetting that constitutes His mercy.

CHAPTER FIVE

Bury Your Weapons

Forgiving Ourselves

"Now therefore be not grieved, nor angry with yourselves."

GENESIS 45:5

"Am I in the Place of God?"

One of the most difficult rooms in the house of forgiveness to enter, ironically, is that titled "Forgiving Ourselves." This room I know very well, but I still wrestle with myself to feel really comfortable in its surroundings. I can withhold forgiveness of myself as well as any man. It can be easier at times to forgive others than to turn that same compassion inward. We believe God and Jesus will forgive, but the stain seems to remain. Like the prodigal, we feel we can never be a son again; servant is sufficient. There is humility in the prodigal's thinking, but a failure to truly understand forgiveness.

We need only return to the brothers of Joseph to understand how enduring guilt over our own behaviors can remain in spite of all assurances from others and from God that the sin has been forgotten. We recall that Joseph had lived in Egypt for thirteen years before his life changed for the better, being seventeen at the time of his slavery and "thirty years old when he stood before Pharaoh" (Genesis 41:46). This was followed by the seven feast years. Sometime in the first or second year of the famine his brothers enter Egypt to buy grain for their families. In time Jacob will be reunited with Joseph and the entire family will move to Egypt. We read that "Jacob lived in the land of Egypt seventeen years" before he died (Genesis 47:28). This gives us roughly thirty-seven or thirty-eight years beyond the brothers' hatred of Joseph that led to his bondage in Egypt. At the death of Jacob, old fears, guilt, and shame resurface. Joseph has lived with his family for seventeen years and yet, in spite of his goodness and the beautiful forgiving reunion when he told them who he was, the sting of their past still hurts. "And when Joseph's brethren saw that their father was dead, they said, Joseph will peradventure hate us, and will certainly requite us all the evil which we did unto him" (Genesis 50:15). That is pure tragedy! They send a messenger to Joseph, telling him, "Thy father did command before he died, saying . . . Forgive, I pray thee now, the trespass of thy brethren, and their sin; for they did unto thee evil: and now, we pray thee, forgive the trespass of the servants of the God of thy father" (Genesis 50:16-17).

The need to forgive was not in Joseph's heart. He had done that years before, and the intervening time should have been sufficient evidence of his sincerity. The difficulty was in the brothers' own hearts, and their thoughts became a barrier to receiving the reassurances and love that Joseph wanted to give. When we cannot forgive ourselves, we have a tendency to project that feeling onto the person or persons we have hurt, which just makes the problem more complex because we still believe we must receive another's forgiveness. In our minds this takes the power out of our hands, when in reality the relief we desire is ours to welcome.

His brothers' message troubled Joseph deeply, especially when they fell before him saying, "Behold, we be thy servants." They are much like the prodigal son who also believed he was no longer worthy of being a son. "And Joseph wept when they spake unto him. . . . And Joseph said unto them, Fear not: for *am I in the place of God?*" (Genesis 50:17–19; emphasis added). That is a good question for us to ask ourselves when we find it hard to forgive our own actions. We are not in the place of God, and if He forgives—and we have seen how easily He does—then we must trust His wiser view and more compassionate judgment. None of us is a proper judge, even of ourselves. Our own assessment of ourselves is rarely reliable. God will do all the judging, for only He sees with pure eyes. When He has forgiven and others have forgiven we do not want to appeal their pardon to the court of our own conscience and return the verdict, "Still guilty!" I have done this in my own life often enough to know the tendency well. I assume you have also. Sometimes we accept the forgiveness and are dealing with the sadness that lingers.

Wisdom

To further reassure his brothers, Joseph acknowledged that what they did was indeed wrong but that God had brought goodness out of it. "As for you, ye thought evil against me; but God meant it unto good," meaning God created goodness out of it (Genesis 50:20). There is wisdom in these words for us also. When self-forgiveness won't come, we can ask ourselves the question, "What good has come out of my past failures?" That may seem a strange question to ask of hurting others, offending God, or harming ourselves, but it is one we must ask. God means for us all to receive *the good of learning* from our choices. That is what the fruit of the tree of the knowledge of good and evil is all about. The good that comes from our misguided choices is *wisdom.* How else can we get it if not from the tree? Healing our soul comes from recognizing the understanding, insight, and knowledge we have gained even from our bad choices and giving up the ache the mortal tutoring has cost us. At least one half of the purpose of that tree of which we all partake is to learn to distinguish between good and evil. That is what makes us like God. The other half is to gain the power to always choose the good. This we will learn in due time. That is more difficult, but we can give ourselves and others some credit for the learning. It can be a painful education, but most learning has its stumbles and failing grades. In school I always wanted the A grade, and life is no different. I suppose not forgiving myself has a little bit to do with those old, school-days feelings. Like Joseph's brothers, we may have thought evil, but God will bring it to good. "Have I learned?" "Are my eyes opened?" The fruit was desirable to make one wise. Are we wise now? At least we are not hiding behind the fig leaves of self-justification or blame. That is a very important acknowledgement and one our society far too often teaches we never need to make. In time both Adam and Eve felt joy. "My eyes are opened," Adam said of his transgression. And Eve added, "We . . . never should have known good and evil" (Moses 5:10–11). "Is there no balm in Gilead?" Jeremiah asked. "Is there no physician there?" (Jeremiah 8:22). That balm is the Savior's love, but it is also the wisdom received, for which we can be grateful; and gratitude and guilt are not compatible companions and can't dwell in the same soul at the same time. We fight our powerlessness before self-condemnation with the balm of learning just as we fight the challenges of forgiving others with the balm of compassion. We battle feelings with more powerful feelings. As I have said, I find it almost impossible to talk my way into self-forgiveness. As in so many areas of the mansion of forgiveness, the soul is a more effective weapon than the mind.

All We Can Do

We suffer sometimes from what could be called "wounditis." The weapon that continues to prick us is an overwrought conscience that can find guilt under every rock, or one that won't let go. When this happens, I turn to a story I have loved for as long as I can remember, but one I had to learn to apply in the room of self-forgiveness. It is that of the converted Lamanites who take the name "Anti-Nephi-Lehies" (see Alma 23:17). Their king gives a most beautiful speech to them as they prepare to face their brothers who have not converted and are preparing to attack them. We all know the decision that is made. They will bury their weapons and never use them again. This is certainly a wonderful story about how to arm ourselves against continuing sin. We try to make it impossible to repeat the offenses by burying the weapons of our past so that in a moment of weakness we will not grab them again. But there is another way of burying the weapons—in this case the ones we use to wound ourselves and keep the sores of our past open and tender. I have used this story over and over again when talking with people who are struggling to forgive themselves.

Notice how the converted Lamanites described themselves! "We were the *most lost of all mankind*" (Alma 24:11; emphasis added). Now there is a wound that requires the balm of Gilead. They had taken life with those swords they buried. I do not think many of us would describe ourselves, no matter how difficult we find it to forgive our past actions, with that designation. *Most lost?* We may have done serious things, but are we the most lost of all mankind? How do you deal with that kind of wound? Three times the king says, "It has been *all that we could do* . . . to get God to take them away from our hearts, for it was *all we could do to repent sufficiently* before God that he would take away our stain. . . . Oh, how merciful is our God! And now behold, since it has been *as much as we could do* to get our stains taken away from us, and our swords are made bright, let us hide them away . . . we will bury them deep in the earth" (Alma 24:11, 15–16; emphasis added).

That is the question we must pose to ourselves. "Have we done all we can do?" (This can be linked with a principle explored earlier. We may have "nothing to pay"—no way of truly making amends.) If the answer is yes (and it is so often when we hold on to the guilt of the past), then let us give Christ His victory. Let us bury the weapons of those former actions that so trouble us instead of holding on to them and using them to continually wound ourselves. I have heard the Spirit ask me many times, "Why do you continue to draw your own sword to your own wounding? Bury it deep in the earth. Let it go." We have done all we can do, just as the woman who wept at the feet of Jesus and dried His feet with her hair. She had done all she could. If we have given the tears, and the hair, and the kiss, and the ointment, and the love, then let us go in peace, as He bids us. He is the example. Remember, He is the Great Forgetter. Bury your weapons knowing, as the Anti-Nephi-Lehies did, that God "loveth our souls as well as he loveth our children" (Alma 24:14). The people "took their swords, and *all the weapons* . . . and they did bury them up deep in the earth" (Alma 24:17; emphasis added). That is good advice. Bury all the weapons of the past! Wisdom is always looking forward, applying the lessons from what went before. What do I know now about the fruits on the tree? What has my experience done to my heart and my soul? Am I nearer to God? Have I learned? I believe that even if we learn on the last second of the last minute of the last hour of the last day, the pains and wounds we inflict even upon ourselves will not have been in vain. Nothing learned in mortality is ever too late. And the learning continues certainly beyond the veil.

Sometimes I try to step into the past as an observer of myself—to put objective distance between me and me. I watch what the teenage Michael did, or the newly married one, or the developing father, or the freshly minted bishop, or the middle-aged Michael. All these Michaels surely did some foolish things and made mistakes; they wounded others and were wounded in kind, but when I look at each Michael with my sixty-five-year-old eyes, I tend to have compassion on him. He was trying. He wanted to do good. Almost always I can see what he learned, and I suspect that the eighty-eight-year-old Michael will feel similar emotions for the sixty-five-year-old man I am now. I also believe the past-death-spirit-world Michael will look back on mortality with the same compassion and understanding.

May I add a final caution? Earlier we examined the parable Jesus told to Simon, a Pharisee, who was distressed that the Lord allowed a woman who had many sins to anoint His feet with ointment. Jesus spoke of two debtors, one who owed five hundred pence and one who owed fifty. Each was duly forgiven, with love the resulting emotion. There are times in my life I can hear the Spirit say to me, "Michael, don't punish yourself with five-hundred-pence pain for fifty-pence offenses." We can overemphasize our own mistakes, and though it sounds a bit self-justifying, our own assessment of the seriousness of our follies is not always reliable. Some may have an overheated conscience. We cure this, as we cure so many things, with forgiveness—forgiveness of ourselves. We can often immerse ourselves in greater guilt, shame, and sorrow than the frailty we have manifested warrants. I believe this is also true of our relations within the family and broader humanity. We must be careful that we don't demand five-hundred-pence apologies, or punishments, or payment, for fifty-pence sins. Too many unnecessary stones have been cast by overwrought and misunderstanding consciences about things that common sense should not call sins, though they may be part of the frailties, weaknesses, and communal humanity of God's children. As the Scottish poet Robert Burns taught, and I am paraphrasing, an honest man has nothing to truly fear in his relationship with God or the coming final accounting, and though he has been the victim or sport of his own instincts, God made those instincts and well knows their power and force better than we do. And what God knows, God will forgive.

Weeds and Rocks

In all things we are asked to emulate our Father and the Savior. What do we know They do with sins when all has been done that can be done? They forget them! They mention them no more! In our desire to be like Them, let us above all things be like Them in this. Let us pray for the grace of God to help us, for forgiveness is always an act of grace and needs grace to reach its fullest liberation. I have read over and over again a letter my wife wrote to me while we were engaged. I turn to it when the weapons of the past continue to wound because I have not buried them deep enough in the earth or when I lay five-hundred-pence anguish upon my fifty-pence failures. I had apologized to Laurie for my insensitivity and for hurting her with my negligence during our engagement. She wrote with wisdom beyond her eighteen years, and her words have power to soothe my soul even now after her passing. She helped me understand the wonder of self-forgiving. "Please don't apologize for those few bad moments," she wrote. "We both learned a lot from them. We still have a lot to learn, but learning is a joy, especially when it is shared. Life won't always be easy for us, as we both well know. We've got a lot of weeds to pull and rocks to throw out of our way yet. But darling, if we stay together through it all and with the Lord guiding our way I know with all my heart that we can stand up to everything. I love you so much for all that you are to me, and for all that you do for me. . . . Please always remember that I love you dearly and need you beside me forever and eternity." And that is how we forgive ourselves!

CHAPTER SIX

When the Soul Is Pierced

Forgiving the Deep Wounds

*"Let not the waterflood overflow me, neither
let the deep swallow me up."*

PSALM 69:15

"With Firmness of Mind"

Each of us will be giving and receiving forgiveness all our lives. That is part of what it means to be human in a mortal state. By the end of life we will have been given sufficient opportunities to practice the art of forgiving. We will gain compassion and wisdom, as has been discussed, bury our weapons, weep with family members, run to the prodigals, and release our debtors. Yet there may be wounds so deep that in spite of all our efforts the relief and healing don't seem to come. Or we nourish the pain and anger because the injury's magnitude appears beyond our abilities to forgive or be forgiven of. Jacob, speaking of the grosser crimes of the men of his generation in regards to their wives and daughters, described their effects with words many may understand: "daggers" had been "placed to pierce their souls and wound their delicate minds. . . . The sobbings of their hearts" had ascended "up to God," and *"many hearts died, pierced with deep wounds"* (Jacob 2:9, 35; emphasis added). That is a haunting phrase! Mormon wrote of the final days of Nephite "depravity . . . perversion" and brutality saying, "The suffering of our women and our children upon all the face of this land doth exceed everything; yea, tongue cannot tell" (Moroni 9:18–19). Here is much to forgive. Abuse, adultery, rebellion, continuing addictions, fraud, and similar acts of betrayal and humiliation may leave lasting scars.

As Jacob counsels in these circumstances, one must "look unto God *with firmness of mind*, and pray unto him with exceeding faith, and he will console you in your affliction, and he will plead your cause. . . . Lift up your heads and receive the pleasing word of God, and feast upon his love; for ye may, *if your minds are firm*, forever" (Jacob 3:1–2; emphasis added). We focus on the verbs in these verses: look, pray, receive, feast. That is our part, and then the promise is that on God's part He will console, plead, love. Eventually He will also "send . . . justice." But our minds must be *firm*. This He repeats twice. This is the phrase that takes the emphasis in Jacob's counsel. Later he speaks of the possibility of being "shaken from . . . *firmness in the Spirit*, and stumble because of . . . over anxiety" (Jacob 4:18; emphasis added). Jacob now adds to firmness of mind a firmness of spirit. I believe and have emphasized that forgiveness is not primarily an act of the mind but one of the soul, yet there is something the mind can do in these most painful trials of our lives. I am blessed in my life in that I have had few, but those few are sufficient to know how very difficult it is to let them go. I can see the necessity of forgiving and continuing forward, acknowledging that holding on to past injuries only harms myself and that forgiveness is primarily about me and not the other person, but the emotions can be so very tenacious. The mind wants justice, and with justice being a quality of goodness, it is hard to argue out the waiving of it. We battle within ourselves—the mind and ego and our pride wanting others to pay, to know what they did to us, and the soul and spirit wanting peace and release and to please God. We live in contradiction, telling others of our injury, which only nourishes it, while hoping they can say or do something to free us from the past and heal the seemingly unhealable wound. We may try to minimize the injury or its pain, but this again is a strategy of the intellect, and some wounds may need to be spoken of, as that is part of the healing process.

When the daggers pierce and the wounds to the heart are deep, the heart may be in danger of dying, as Jacob suggests. The firm mind, with the supporting firmness of spirit, must help, but how? In my own life, reversing a very common statement has been of immeasurable value. We have all heard the phrase, "I will forgive, but I won't forget." We all recognize a bit of hypocrisy in that idea, but at some level it is true. We can forgive, release the negative feelings, try to regain trust, but the memory remains as an echo of sorrow if nothing else. However, I think the proper phrase to begin with is, "I will forget, since I cannot forgive." When I think of the injury, *I hurt.* So I must stop thinking of it. That is a logical conclusion. In that necessity the mind can be firm. I have gone to my Father in Heaven, as Jacob suggested, and prayed for Him to console and love, to plead for me and grant the pleasing words. I have feasted on His words and felt the flow of His forgiving stories, but there are times when the pain is still too great. In these times I have said to Him, "Father, I wish to forgive. I don't want the negativity and the self-pity to remain. I don't want to want the person who hurt me to pay with equal suffering, but I can't get there. I will give you what I can. I will give you forgetfulness. I will not think of the past injury. I will not feed it by dwelling on it but will push it back, as I should with all unworthy thoughts." This is what the mind can do. This is how the mind can help.

Is this not what the Lord does when He tells us He will forget our sins and not mention them? I used to think this forgetting applied only after repentance, but now I realize that for you and me it may be necessary before the forgiveness. It may be all we can do. I have never felt that the Lord was not pleased with this approach. It may not be the full step we desire, but it is a step, and I believe it will in time bring the heart's forgiveness also. Elder Richard G. Scott further emphasized that the Lord will accept whatever offering we are capable of when the wound is too grievous to immediately forgive: "While an important part of healing, if the thought of forgiveness causes you yet more pain, set that step aside until you have more experience with the Savior's healing power in your own life" ("To Heal the Shattering Consequences of Abuse," *Ensign*, May 2008, 42–43).

For me, Jacob's suggestion that the mind be firm holds this within its meaning. It means other things as well, such as not letting the injuries destroy one's life in depression, guilt, shame, anger, or a feeling of helplessness. The mind is a great tool. Though it may not be able to produce forgiveness, it can control what it thinks. So we close the door every time the deep wounds cry for attention and try to engage in another area of the house. "I cannot yet forgive, so I will forget." In one sense, is this not what forgiveness is? If we were the one who did the injury, and, as we talked about in the last chapter, have done all we can do, then forgetfulness is also part of the mercy we receive from God and from ourselves.

There is a part of me that believes if I just think and talk long enough about a problem I will discover a way to eliminate it. I will be able to produce a state of forgiveness. I have a great deal of trust in the mind's capacities, but in this area, I have to go against my instincts and let the will tell the mind that we will not debate, argue, search, and reason for some mental solution. Instead, we will cease thinking about the episode. We will forget, because I can't reason my way into believing that pain is not pain and wounds are not so deep or so bad. I can't heal the soul with the mind's resources. The mind gravitates naturally to justice. It makes more sense. I can't think myself into the joy of forgiveness. But I can turn the mind. I can focus it. I can forget.

The thoughts that may be most helpful to foster are loving thoughts, or those that help create a loving spirit, for we must always remember that love is a stronger emotion than any negative one that wishes to challenge it. The mind wants to feed on something, so we will redirect it away from pain and into love—love for anything. I am aware of someone who found a measure of healing and the ability to overcome the memories of past abusive situations through the love of a dog. This was a conscious choice of fruits from the tree of knowledge of good and evil. In a world that can shatter us with its cruelty, pettiness, selfishness, and injustice, we can choose love and mercy and wisdom. If we do not, we risk being overcome by the very powers that hurt us, for hate and resentment and bitterness and vengeance are definitely equal to themselves. They *can* be a defense—an ointment that will ease pain for a while—but they are a defense that ultimately destroy what they defend. We pray and plead with firmness of spirit that compassion be found in our heart, for the charity that "seeketh not her own . . . thinketh no evil . . . *beareth all things, believeth all things, hopeth all things, endureth all things*" (1 Corinthians 13:4-7; emphasis added). This is what, with firmness of mind, we pray the grace of God will help us achieve. That is the prayer part of Jacob's counsel. We must be humble enough to ask for it, and that is often the first step in letting go of past injuries. We must want to let go enough to sincerely pray that we can. I grew up watching my mother do this very thing. The divorce gave her a great deal of pain, as well as feelings of betrayal and anger. But she focused all her energies and thoughts on her three children. Her thoughts were, therefore, loving thoughts, and though she was our salvation, in a way we were hers. Charity and compassion are how Jesus endured all that the world could put upon Him, as Nephi testified: "The world . . . shall judge him to be a thing of naught; wherefore they scourge him, and he suffereth it; and they smite him, and he suffereth it. Yea, they spit upon him, and he suffereth it, because of his loving kindness" (1 Nephi 19:9).

Silver in the Temple

I can think of no scripture story more poignant in its example of a person in such despair that he felt forgiveness was impossible than that of Judas Iscariot. Here is a man who cannot forgive himself, and I assume he believed Jesus could not forgive him either. His deep wound was self-inflicted, as many are. Judas had his problems before the betrayal. He complained about Mary anointing the Savior prior to Jesus' hour, for wasting an expensive gift that might have been used to bless the poor. This brought from John the statement, "This he said, not that he cared for the poor; but because he was a thief, and had the bag, and bare what was put therein" (John 12:6). At the Last Supper, Jesus was "troubled in spirit" when He testified that one of the disciples would betray Him (John 13:21). As for the placement of the story of Judas, Matthew relates Judas' repentance immediately after telling us that Peter, remembering the words of Jesus that he would deny Him, "went out, and wept bitterly" (Matthew 26:75). That scene sets the stage for Judas. Two Apostles would weep bitterly that day. "Then Judas . . . when he saw that he was condemned, *repented himself,* and brought again the thirty pieces of silver to the chief priests and elders, saying, I have sinned in that I have betrayed the innocent blood. And they said, What is that to us? see thou to that" (Matthew 27:3–4; emphasis added). We would not be so unfeeling. Their callousness only serves to heighten the tragedy of Judas' too-late regrets. Fortunately, I do not believe that is ever the Savior's or His Father's attitude. Yet, weighed down with the immensity of what he had done, Judas "cast down the pieces of silver in the temple, and departed, and went and hanged himself" (Matthew 27:5). That is tragedy, and I find myself weeping for Judas. Here is one who is truly "most lost of all mankind." I love the Savior. I feel deeply His passion, and the pain and perfidy of the betrayal is a wounding moment on the consciousness of the world. Yet Jesus had called Judas "friend" even in the act of betrayal in the Garden of Gethsemane. We get some idea of what the Savior felt toward Judas' betrayal in the Psalms: "For it was not an enemy that reproached me; then I could have borne it: neither was it he that hated me . . . then I would have hid myself from him: but it was thou, a man mine equal, my guide, and mine acquaintance. We took sweet counsel together, and walked into the house of God in company" (Psalm 55:12–14).

Perhaps the greatest sadness about Judas was the depth of his agony, which would admit no glimmer of hope for himself, no trust that even in this, perhaps his God could find an answer in mercy. George MacDonald wrote: "But must we believe that Judas, who repented even to agony, who repented so that his high-prized life, self, soul, became worthless in his eyes and met with no mercy at his own hand—must we believe that he could find no mercy in such a God? I think, when Judas fled from his hanged and fallen body, he fled to the tender help of Jesus, and found it. . . . Jesus loved Judas even when he was kissing him with the traitor's kiss; and I believe that he was his Savior still" (*Unspoken Sermons*, 53). Jesus would certainly keep His own rules, His counsels to us. Did He not teach us to "love your enemies, bless them that curse you, do good to them that hate you, and pray for them which despitefully use you, and persecute you; that ye may be the children of your Father which is in heaven"? (Matthew 5:44–45). In Luke's account of these words, he ends with, "Be ye therefore merciful, as your Father also is merciful" (Luke 6:36). Let that mercy be directed to ourselves, especially when we "cast down the pieces of silver in the temple." Let it be directed to those who have betrayed us, knowing they too will one day scatter their coins on the floor.

CHAPTER SEVEN

Is There No Pity?

Forgiving God

"My desire is, that the Almighty would answer me."

JOB 31:35

Talk with Me of Thy Judgments

In one of William Shakespeare's most beloved plays, *Romeo and Juliet*, his heroine turns her eyes to heaven when all have abandoned her and cries, "Is there no pity sitting in the clouds that sees into the bottom of my grief? . . . Alack, alack, that heaven should practice stratagems upon so soft a subject as myself!" (Act III, scene V, lines 198–199, 211–212). In other plays, Macduff in *Macbeth* wonders how God could have looked on at the murder of his wife and children without helping, and Elizabeth in *Richard the III* lamenting the murder of her two sons can only wonder why God slept when the deed was done. Shakespeare was only one great mind and soul who questioned God due to the miseries and apparent indifference of heaven toward the helpless. Some of the greatest prophets have also wondered why a just God would allow such pain and suffering to overwhelm so many of His children. "Righteous art thou, O Lord, when I plead with thee," prayed Jeremiah, "yet let me talk with thee of thy judgments:

Wherefore doth the way of the wicked prosper?" (Jeremiah 12:1). Habakkuk asked why God had made "men as the fishes of the sea . . . that have no ruler over them?" (Habakkuk 1:14). Are we really at the mercy of the law of the jungle? Are we alone in a friendless universe? People from Job to Dostoevsky, from Eli Wiesel to Joseph Smith wrestled with an omnipotent, benevolent God who allows man to perpetrate such horrible atrocities on his fellow man and allows nature to exact such painful, seemingly unnecessary and mindless diseases, disasters, and famines. And, of course, there is even Jesus' cry from Calvary, "My God, my God, why hast thou forsaken me?" (Mark 15:34). Many respond with anger at God, at the world, and let faith die—not always out of apathy, but out of anguish at what they perceive is strong evidence against a loving God. C. S. Lewis turned atheist for a number of reasons, one of them being his belief that no matter what he did he could not satisfy God and another being the cruelty of the world around him. "I maintained that God did not exist. I was also very angry with God for not existing. I was equally angry with Him for creating a world" (*Surprised by Joy* [Harcourt, Inc., 1955], 115).

Sometimes being angry at God can come very close to home. I am grateful that His dignity and understanding can withstand a few judgmental eyes looking heavenward, for my own have so looked. I also remember my helplessness in providing for my son an answer when he openly and poignantly said at the death of his mother, "I'm trying not to be mad at God, but why would He take my mother?" It may be boldness bordering on impertinence to speak of "forgiving God," but sometimes that is a need that some people feel. These emotions may be somewhat misplaced, but they are real enough not to be dismissed. Can one forgive God? Technically, no, as He never sins, but for some the dilemma is pressing, and anger at God for the trials of life is a very common sentiment. We can and should at least tell Him what is in our hearts. He knows anyway, and He always desires face-to-face conversations. We must not be evasive with God. We go to great efforts to explain God and give satisfying answers to pain and suffering, but obviously none of them are sufficient or we would stop asking the questions. I wish for my own sake I could comfort everyone from Juliet to Jeremiah, but I know no answer. Believe me, I have tried to put these things to rest. I have tried to find words to release the anger at God that I have encountered in many people, from my best friend in youth who went to Vietnam to students or members of my ward or stake. There is a strong voice inside me that urges me not to even try to deal with this topic, as I know I will come short; nevertheless, there is a room in the mansion of forgiveness devoted to forgiving or reconciling with God, so let us enter and see what we can learn.

Transcend!

In the room there is one main thought that has helped me: we cannot always explain God or understand His ways concerning this world, but we can transcend the evil around us and rise in goodness. Instead of discussing, we act—and we act in compassion knowing others also are so doing. We can prove by our lives that the positive virtues of love, kindness, mercy, patience, service, and gentleness are greater than any combination of negatives that we may come to experience or know. People often ask, "How can we make sense of such a world, a world of genocide, child abuse, brutality, mass murders, school shootings, suicide bombers, and perversion? How can any good God let such things exist, which have existed throughout time?" I can't make sense of it, can you? I have tried to respond with my head, with my reason, but it fails me every time, though some explanations are offered that give a little relief. We must respond, as in so many of the rooms of forgiveness, with our hearts and souls. Evil is out there. Cruelty has always existed and will continue. These things happen to millions and they happen to us. But we cannot let the outside forces that push so painfully against the soul overwhelm it. We transcend it all. We learn to respond to the world the way Jesus did, with love and trust. "In the world ye shall have tribulation," Jesus said in the last hours of His life, "but be of good cheer; I have overcome the world" (John 16:33). How did He overcome the world? With love, compassion, kindness, faith, sacrifice, pity, empathy, mercy, and yes, sorrow—with tears. That is the key to this room. We must also remember that we do have one powerful image of God as He looks upon the wickedness of the world, related by Enoch in Moses chapter 7. That wickedness will lead to their destruction in the flood. We are told the wicked had filled the earth with "violence" (Moses 8:28). That is a word our modern world understands. Yet the Father wept over their eventual suffering. Though "Satan shall be their father," yet Jesus would plead for them and suffer for their sins (Moses 7:37–39). Peter and Joseph F. Smith both taught that it is these violent, wicked people for whom

Is There No Pity?

Jesus instituted the preaching of the gospel in the spirit world (see 1 Peter 3:18-20; D&C 138). That is mercy beyond my comprehension when I contemplate the violent actions of my own time. God always responds with love and forgiveness if it can be given, and it seems that in almost all situations it can.

Instead of trying to explain God or justify His ways, we will try to emulate the Father's qualities as they were shown to us by His Son. The world is not always reasonable. In truth it defies reason at times. But there is something deep inside us that believes love balances, and even outweighs, the evil we cannot avoid or eliminate. The best-living man in history suffered all the indignities of the world, responding always in love, and no man loved God more greatly or had more faith in His goodness. He would not jump off the pinnacle of the temple at the suggestion of Lucifer because He did not believe God had to prove anything to Him. The way He lived and what He believed are related. We must believe that living like Christ eventually results in an understanding of the Father's ways as Jesus understood them. Sometimes we think that confirmation of belief comes first and then we live according to those beliefs. I would suggest that is somewhat backward. Instead, let us live as did Jesus. Let us be compassionate, forgiving, and kind, and then the assurance of a like-minded God will come and the crisis of faith will diminish. There will be no need to forgive God. His ways are self-justifying when we live them. Overcome the world, Jesus taught us with His life, as I have done, by transcending its negatives with all that is best within you.

The Peaceable Followers of Christ

During those chaotic, "awful brutality . . . depravity . . . without order and without mercy . . . strong in their perversion" days at the end of Nephite civilization, Mormon addressed a group who in his mind merited special consideration (Moroni 9:17–19). Mormon called these people "the peaceable followers of Christ." He told them that he gave them this designation "because of [their] peaceable walk with the children of men." Through the goodness of their lives, in spite of the terrible world in which they lived, they had "obtained a sufficient hope by which ye can enter into the rest of the Lord, from this time henceforth until ye shall rest with him in heaven" (Moroni 7:3–4). Notice that they would have rest in *this* world, not just wait for it to come in the next. What counsel does Mormon share with those living in a world that can cause one to doubt and even be angry at God for all they see and experience? The key ideas and words in Mormon's address are powerful and relevant. Here are just a few. They were to "judge," "search diligently," "lay hold," and "cleave unto *every good thing*" (Moroni 7:16, 19, 28; emphasis added). Even in that brutal world there was still much goodness to discover. They were counseled to search for it. Take hold of it. Never let it go. This they would do by the grace of the light of Christ, by His example and gifts. They were to have "a firm mind in every form of godliness" (Moroni 7:30). There is our firmness again. The most essential qualities of that godliness were "faith," "meekness," "lowly of heart," "hope," and above all things, "charity . . . the pure love of Christ" (Moroni 7:33, 39, 41, 43, 45–48). There follow the qualities that define charity, which mirror those described by Paul in 1 Corinthians chapter 13—long-suffering, kindness, selflessness, humility, mildness, joy in truth, endurance. The obtaining of these virtues, especially against the backdrop of the evil of the society surrounding them, made them the "true followers of his Son, Jesus Christ." They could be "like him . . . purified even as he is pure" (Moroni 7:48).

Mormon's words give us the pattern for living in a harsh world. They testify to the hope that one can transcend even the most cruel and violent of surroundings or unexplainable events in our own lives, which may tempt us to disbelieve in a loving Father. The life Mormon describes is its own witness. Live it and you will see, he promises us over the centuries that separate us. The placing of the book of Ruth right after the horrible ugliness of the last chapters of the book of Judges gives the same message. In a world where humanity can be so inhuman, there will always be the gentle, loving, unselfish kindness of such people as Ruth, Naomi, and Boaz. We surely need to believe in God, but we can also believe in humanity, because such people are in it. If we find ourselves angry at the world and its Creator, let us look for the "peaceable followers of Christ," for the Ruths and the Naomis, and in the beauty of their lives believe in the Being that inspires them. Let us be such souls ourselves—part of the solution and not part of the problem. What happens to us in the end is almost always less important than how we respond to what happens to us. The main question may not be, "What is God going to do about all this evil and suffering?" but, "What am I going to do about it?" Even if the worst fears about God were true, it would change nothing about how we are to act. Here we have examples to follow, the greatest being our Savior, but with

Him are many ordinary men and women who believe love and forgiveness have more power than cruelty.

Redeemed from All Evil

If there were individuals in Mormon's generation who transcended their age through seeking the good and holding firm in every form of godliness, we receive a more personal example in the life of Jacob in Genesis. Though the society of Genesis was not as degenerate as Mormon's, it was a dangerous society nonetheless, both spiritually and physically. If we have suffered from a world that defies justice and reason and tempts or persuades us to hold God responsible for not changing the disorder of our lives, Jacob had similar reasons. Look at his life. His brother is favored by his father. Esau threatens to kill him. He's separated from his mother, Rebekah, and father, Isaac, for twenty years. Laban beguiles him. He's married to a woman he does not love. His family is in almost constant conflict. His beloved Rachel is for many years barren and then dies in her youth giving birth to Benjamin. He mourns her all his life. Dinah, his daughter, is ravished by the Canaanites. His sons Simeon and Levi are murderers, treacherously slaughtering the men of Shechem. Judah has children by a Canaanite woman—we are not told if he married her—and then conceives sons by his daughter-in-law, thinking she is a harlot. One of his grandsons, Er, is so wicked we are told God slew him. His wife, Bilhah, is defiled by his own son, Reuben, whom he heartbreakingly called "the excellency of dignity" (Genesis 49:3). Joseph, his most worthy son, is thought dead—killed by wild beasts. He faces the extinction of his family by famine. He lives his last years in an alien country knowing his descendants will eventually be enslaved there. Think how much could have been avoided had Jacob only been born first. Mere minutes separated his birth with that of Esau. That troublesome birthright! Where is the justice in this? If God wanted Jacob to carry the birthright, why not bring him from the womb first and avoid half the problems? Yet God loved Jacob. Though he would say at a low point in his life, "All these things are against me" (Genesis 42:36), at the end of his life, gazing backward with the perspective of old age, Jacob would praise God. While blessing Joseph's two sons, Jacob said, "God, before whom my fathers Abraham and Isaac did walk, the God which fed me all my life long unto this day. The Angel which *redeemed me from all evil*, bless the lads" (Genesis 48:15-16; emphasis added). We might be tempted to say of Jacob's life that God had *not* redeemed him from all evil, but that was not Jacob's conclusion. Somehow, through it all, he never lost the ground of his faith. Perhaps William Tyndale, the great Bible translator and reformer, summed up his life's lessons best when he wrote, "They that be strong therefore must suffer with the weak" (Wilcox, *Fire in the Bones* [Deseret Book, 2004], 133).

We too must be strong—strong in faith, in hope, in goodness, and above all in compassion and forgiveness. Jacob had much to forgive, and in his own weaknesses to be forgiven of, but he rose above it all. We learn to trust in God above all appearances, in spite of all realities. We learn that God does not always explain His ways to us; He appeals to our childheart and awakens our love so we may trust. We learn that though mankind is but the dust of the earth, it is dust worth the agonies of Gethsemane and the death of the cross. It is dust that can forgive. We are dust that God believes will still love and honor Him even against the evidence of a troubled world, and that is high praise. Perhaps the great question is not, "How can we continue to believe in God in light of the sorrow and turmoil of all we see?" but, "How can God continue to believe in us?" Yet He does! That is the height of His beauty—the beauty of forgiveness.

The Beauty of Forgiving and Forgiveness

"Mercy hath compassion on mercy and claimeth her own."

DOCTRINE & COVENANTS 88:40

F orgiveness is such a lovely thing—most beautiful in a gospel of magnificent beauty. Perhaps it lifts itself even a fraction above the simple wonder of loving compassion, as it involves injury and hurt—compassion squared by personal pain, not only empathetic understanding and love. It asks the most of the human soul. I have received forgiveness and have been asked to bestow it. Both are equally joyous, equally divine. William Shakespeare, who understood mercy, compassion, and forgiveness as well as any man I've read, described the joy and wonder of forgiving and receiving forgiveness this way:

> The quality of mercy is not strained,
> It droppeth as the gentle rain from heaven
> Upon the place beneath. It is twice blest;
> It blesseth him that gives and him that takes. . . .
> It is an attribute to God himself. . . .
> We do pray for mercy,
> And that same prayer doth teach us all to render
> The deeds of mercy.
>
> (The Merchant of Venice, Act IV, scene I, lines 184–202; emphasis added)

Twice Blessed

As with all aspects of the gospel, forgiveness is much deeper and more beautiful than we appreciate on our first examinations. It has taken me a lifetime to begin to understand and practice such principles as "coming near," "loosing the debtor," "seeing the woman," or being clothed with forgiveness from the very gates of Eden. We are told in the scriptures that one day, if we can prove worthy, we will be invited to sit upon God's own throne, ruling and reigning as kings and queens. That throne has a name. It is called the mercy seat. We sing of it in one of our most beloved hymns. It is the defining quality of our Father in Heaven and His Son, and we would be like Them. Our Father in Heaven rules worlds without number from a throne of mercy and forgiveness. Until we sit with Him in glory on a future eternal morning, let us try as best we can to rest comfortably upon earthly mercy seats in the much smaller worlds of our own relationships. I am far from mastering the art of forgiving and forgiveness, but their beauty draws me on. It is a beauty that is fair as the moon. Surely we never tire of seeing that soft and gentle light. May forgiveness shine in full-moon splendor in your heart and in mine.

Index

Index

Index

Index